PRIVATE SECURITY

PRIVATE SECURITY
A Canadian Perspective

ROBERT J. GERDEN

Prentice Hall Canada Career & Technology
Scarborough, Ontario

Canadian Cataloguing in Publication Data

Gerden, Robert J.
   Private Security : a Canadian perspective

Includes index.
ISBN 0-13-693426-9

1. Private security services - Canada. 2. Police, Private - Canada. I. Title.

HV8291.C3G46 1998   363.2'89'0971   C97-932104-2

 © 1998 Prentice-Hall Canada Inc., Scarborough, Ontario
A Division of Simon & Schuster/A Viacom Company

Prentice-Hall, Inc., Upper Saddle River, New Jersey
Prentice-Hall International (UK) Limited, London
Prentice-Hall of Australia, Pty. Limited, Sydney
Prentice-Hall Hispanoamericana, S.A., Mexico City
Prentice-Hall of India Private Limited, New Delhi
Prentice-Hall of Japan, Inc., Tokyo
Simon & Schuster Southeast Asia Private Limited, Singapore
Editora Prentice-Hall do Brasil, Ltda., Rio de Janeiro

Photo Credits: p.22, Intercon Security; p. 89, Marineland (top), Bank of Montreal
(middle and bottom); p. 90, Newbridge Networks (top), Northern Telecom (middle),
TRW Automotive (bottom); p. 91, Sears Canada (left), Intercon Security (right).

ISBN 0-13-693426-9

Vice President, Editorial Director: Laura Pearson
Acquisitions Editor: David Stover
Executive Marketing Manager: Jo-Ann DeLuca
Production Editor: Andrew Winton
Copy Editor: Matthew Kudelka
Production Coordinator: Leora Conway
Permissions/Photo Research: Susan Wallace-Cox
Cover Design: Monica Kompter
Cover Image: PhotoDisc
Page Layout: Arlene Edgar

1 2 3 4 5   RRD   02 01 00 99 98

Printed and bound in the United States of America.

Visit the Prentice Hall Canada web site! Send us your comments, browse our catalogues, and more
at **www.phcanada.com**. Or reach us through e-mail at **phabinfo_pubcanada@prenhall.com**.

To my family

Contents

CHAPTER 4: RISK MANAGEMENT/ ASSET PROTECTION   81

Preface

The purpose of this book is to provide the reader with information about private security trends and issues, legal authority, and career opportunities. The perspective taken here will be specifically Canadian. In law and security courses I have taught, my students often ask the same questions about the field; in this book, I will try to answer many of them. In doing so I hope to provide the reader with a knowledge foundation—and perhaps even a mental framework—for approaching the private security industry. Private security has changed over the years, and I hope this book will dispel a number of outdated stereotypes about the profession.

Private security is a growing industry. Those who want to tap into this growth, especially at the high end, should be aware of the many possible alternatives for entering the field. I will try to present the information in an objective fashion, but I would encourage the reader to apply a healthy degree of skepticism when considering opinions regarding such matters as education, career paths, and employment opportunities.

I would add that the information in this book should not be construed as legal advice, but rather as a basis for further discussion and research. One should seek out expert opinion, legal or otherwise, for any particular situation.

In closing, I would like to offer a special thanks to the following people for their time and advice: Ed Burgie, Bob Diguer, Norman Inkster, David L. Ray, and David Stover. Thanks also to those who reviewed the manuscript, including Jeff Agro (Seneca College), Dan Overy (Lambton College), J.E. Judd (Durham College), and Dennis M. Roughley (Georgian College). I would like to add a special thanks to Jeannie Arsenault for her continuous support and counsel. She is not only a great writer and editor, but also my mother-in-law.

About the Author

Robert Gerden taught postsecondary courses in law and security for several years, including courses in investigations and casino security. He also worked for the federal and Ontario provincial departments of the Solicitor General; while with these departments, he developed reports for the policing and security branches and proferred advice on a variety of issues, including public and private policing as well as national security. Mr. Gerden holds a degree in criminology and public policy and management from the University of Ottawa and is currently pursuing his master's degree in criminal justice at Niagara University. He is now employed as an investigator with Lindquist, Avey, Macdonald, Baskerville, an international forensic and investigative accounting firm.

WHAT IS PRIVATE SECURITY?

1

CHAPTER OBJECTIVES

- Define private security.
- Understand how private security is organized in Canada.
- Identify types of security services and products.
- Analyze the growth and revenue of the private security industry.
- Identify reasons for the growth of the private security industry.
- Define certain private security positions.

Worldwide, the field of private security is growing tremendously. The number of private security personnel in Canada is difficult to estimate (see below), but recent studies suggest it is in the neighbourhood of 200 000. For comparative purposes, Statistics Canada has estimated the number of sworn public police officers (federal, provincial, and municipal) to be close to 56 000. Both estimates are open to debate, mainly because definitions are fluid, but the point I am making still holds—private security is clearly a much larger field than public policing. General estimates of money spent in each industry are $3 billion for private security and almost $6 billion for public policing. Thus, there are far more workers in private security, but these workers cost less by as much as half.

By all indicators, the field of private security is going to continue to grow. Despite its emphasis on hardware and technology instead of personnel, the security industry will continue to provide a variety of job opportunities. The average person, when asked to conjure an image of private security, used to picture—and to a certain extent still pictures—a lonely security guard, usually a retiree, sitting at a desk watching an entrance point. In fact, the security industry is extremely diverse: there are still plenty of security guards, but there are also computer security experts, forensic accountants, executive protection specialists, alarm manufacturers and installers, and locksmiths. Many people do not see just how large the industry really is.

HISTORY OF PRIVATE SECURITY

There has always been private security. In ancient times people relied mainly on physical measures such as cliffs, moats, drawbridges, and walls. In the Middle Ages societies began developing a collective responsibility for maintaining law and order. This collective responsibility evolved to the point where many citizens were given the power to arrest and complemented the state-appointed constables by patrolling the city with them at night (this was known as the "watch and ward" system). The "hue and cry" and the "assize of arms" were two other systems in place during this time. In the former, the "watchman" (that is, the private citizen) cried out for his fellow citizens to join him in the pursuit of a fugitive. This led to assize of arms laws being passed requiring all male citizens between 15 and 60 to have a weapon in the home in the event they were needed to help maintain law and order. Clearly, citizens took an active role at the time in protecting persons and property, since they could not rely on government protection, such as a public police force.

The next major development in law enforcement was in the mid-nineteenth century, when Sir Robert Peel, the British home secretary, helped enact the Metropolitan Police Act, which in turn created the London Metropolitan Police. Peel's approach involved crime prevention through community responsibility; it also involved hiring civilians from the community as full-time police officers. Peel's famous dictum was that "the police are the public and the public are the police." However, Hess and Wrobleski (1992) have pointed out that the police forces of Peel's time were more *reactive* to crimes (as opposed to proactive) than their founder intended. It was private security that would fulfil the need for *proactive* security.

In the United States, private security grew in importance and visibility as the railroads expanded west in the mid-1800s. There was no national police force, and there were very few local police forces, yet the railroads still needed to protect their people and goods, and private security firms emerged to fill this need. Listed in Table 1.1 are some important milestones in the American private security industry.

These firms later expanded to fill niches such as cash transportation, alarm manufacturing and maintenance, business property protection, and strike-breaking. Many of the companies listed above are still in existence today.

In Canada, as in the United States, the private security industry came into being because there were no public police forces. Stenning and Cornish (1975) point out that there were no salaried police in Ontario until 1875 and that by 1903 there were still only six full-time police officers in the province. The first police officer in Ontario was previously the head of detectives for the Canadian Southern Railway. Private security in Canada, as in the United States, was born with the railroads.

TABLE 1.1	Early Private Security Firms
Pinkerton National Detective Agency (1851)	Protection of railroad assets.
Wells Fargo and Company (1852)	Transportation of goods.
North West Police Agency (1855)	Protection of railroad assets.
Pinkerton Protection Patrol (1857)	Provision of contract security personnel.
Holmes Protection, Inc. (1858)	Provision of central burglar alarms.
Brink's, Inc. (1858)	Transportation of goods.
William J. Burns Detective Agency (1909)	Provision of contract security personnel.
Wackenhut Corporation (1954)	Provision of contract security personnel.

DEFINITION

There is no standard definition of private security in Canada—or anywhere else, for that matter. This is why it is important for readers to know from the outset how statisticians define certain terms when they study the security industry, since those definitions can obviously influence the numbers they gather and report. In the simplest terms: Be cautious when viewing statistics.

Do we count as private security personnel those employees for whom security duties are only perhaps 10 percent of their work? For these workers, the other 90 percent may be totally unrelated to security work. Perhaps, for example, a receptionist is watching an entrance while otherwise performing clerical duties, or a teacher is spending some time supervising a dance. Shearing and colleagues (1980) suggest that private security personnel have the following attributes:

- They are employed in jobs whose principal component is a security function.
- They are privately employed.
- They are privately accountable.
- They have no special powers to maintain the peace.

However, this definition does not account for those public police whom private organizations can hire as off-duty officers (such as for major league baseball games). These authors further suggest that it might be convenient to place public and private security on a continuum, with public police (who have full peace-officer status) at one end, and private security workers (who have no peace-officer status and who are under private control) at the other end. Off-duty police, or special constables (such as CN police) hired by nongovernment organizations, would thus fall somewhere between these two ends of the spectrum.

Some definitions tend to exclude certain categories of private security. For example, the U.S. Private Security Task Force defined private security as follows (1976): "Private security includes those self-employed individuals and privately funded business entities and organizations providing security-related services to specific clientele for a fee, for the individual or entity that retains or employs them, or for themselves, in order to protect their persons, private property, or interests from various hazards."

Likewise, Smith and Prouse (1987) limited the concept of private security by defining it as "the method of protecting one's assets, be they individual or corporate, through total loss prevention techniques, and having this protection paid for by a nongovernmental body" (p. 2). Both the above definitions would *not* include private security personnel who provide protection services to governments and get paid in tax dollars (for example, members of the Canadian Corps of Commissionaires, who protect federal buildings, or the House of Commons guards).

Other definitions tend to exclude the sector of the industry that manufactures, distributes, and installs security hardware. Note this definition, from Gion Green (1981): "Private security can be defined as those individuals, organizations, and services, other than public law enforcement agencies, which are engaged primarily in the prevention of crime, loss, or harm to specific individuals, organizations, or facilities."

The following definition corrects many of the above deficiencies: "Private security is a profit-oriented industry that provides personnel, equipment, and/or procedures to prevent losses caused by human error, emergencies, disasters, or criminal actions" (Hess and Wrobleski, 1992: 27). Yet again, this definition excludes certain categories, such as "volunteer" security for a special event (perhaps a school sporting event).

Finally, there is this definition, proposed in 1996 at the Second Conference of the Canadian Security Sector. This one, perhaps, is the most inclusive: "The security sector is an essential component in crime prevention, investigation, and protection of all people, assets and property. It involves all those who have an interest in, a concern for, and are beneficiaries of security. It is both a provider of security services and security goods (equipment). It includes all the stakeholders: owners, employees and organized labour; governments, corporations and businesses; educators, standards organizations and associations. It is both dedicated (in-house) and for hire (contract)."

Whichever definition of private security we use, it must be flexible enough to incorporate both personnel and technological aspects. It must also distinguish between public police and private security and those in between. Also, private security no longer concerns itself merely with preventing crime. Thus, it is now commonly associated with—if not fully integrated with—areas such as risk management, with risk being defined as anything that could hurt profits. Such risk could relate to human error (which could trigger lawsuits), or natural disasters (such as flooding), or other types of emergencies. As a result of this widening role, many security departments are being renamed "loss prevention" or "resource protection" departments.

TYPES OF SECURITY SERVICES AND PRODUCTS

Clearly, the private security industry is a diverse one. This diversity is reflected in the following lists of security services and security products available in Canada. These lists are based largely on work by Leclair and Long (1996) and are by no means exclusive. Rather, they are meant to indicate the wide range of positions and products that fall under this large industry. New niches are constantly being created to meet market demand. Some of the following categories may overlap with each other (for example, alarm installing and monitoring).

Security Services

- Airport security
- Alarm installation and repair
- Alarm monitoring
- Armoured car services
- Bodyguards
- Consultants
- Corporate security
- Court security
- Drug testing
- Executive protection
- Fire prevention
- Forensic analysis
- Forensic accounting
- Guard dogs
- Honesty testing
- House protection
- Information security
- Investigations
- Locksmiths
- Paid off-duty police officers (despite off-duty police officers still being considered peace officers, they are essentially under the direction of a private enterprise)
- Patrol guards, mobile patrols—alarm response
- Polygraph specialist
- Prison security (contracted to private firms such as the Wackenhut Corporation)
- Security engineering
- Security guards
- Security insurance underwriting
- Security market research
- Security publishing
- Security storage
- Security training/education
- Special constables (depending on who the employer is)
- Uniform rentals

Security Products (manufacturing and distribution)

- Access control
- Armoured car
- Audio monitors and submersible phones
- Barriers
- Bomb disposal suits
- Burglar alarm systems
- Bullet-proof clothing
- Closed Circuit Television (CCTV)
- Computer security shielding
- Detection devices; explosives/ bomb/narcotics/metal/weapon
- Electronic ID
- Encryption software
- Fire alarm systems
- G-suits, cold water survival suits
- Locks/safes/vaults
- Personal alarms
- Plastics formation
- Polygraph equipment
- Robots
- Rubber/silicon formation
- Security fencing/perimeter detectors and fences
- Security lighting
- Surveillance equipment
- Telephone equipment
- Tempest casing
- Water disrupter

IN-HOUSE VERSUS CONTRACT

The private security industry can be further divided into two components: in-house and contract. *In-house* (or proprietary) security consists of organizations that hire and pay for their own security personnel. These personnel have only one employer and protect the assets of only that employer. The retail and banking sectors (Sears, the Royal Bank, and so on) rely mainly on in-house security. *Contract* security refers to organizations that provide security services to clients on a contractual basis. An employee of a contract security firm may provide services to a variety of clients throughout his or her career. Pinkerton, Burns, Loomis, Group 4, and Intercon are all contract security organizations.

It is important to note that many companies use in-house and contract security at the same time: the two options are not mutually exclusive. Typically, when the two categories are combined, there is an in-house director or manager of security who outsources to contract security companies a number of security tasks (for example, he or she will hire a private investigation company to conduct a specialized fraud investigation). General Motors uses this combined approach: there is usually an in-house security manager who oversees the contracting of security guards from Pinkerton.

There are advantages and disadvantages (both real or perceived) to both contract and in-house security. Hess and Wrobleski (1992) summarized these as they were put forward in a 1976 American study, *Task Force Report on Private Security* (Private Security, 1976: 245–246). However, these pros and cons are open to question, since there has been little recent empirical research to validate them. The lists in Table 1.2 are provided as a basis for discussion *only*—depending on the circumstances, one could very well argue the exact opposite of many of these points.

TABLE 1.2	In-house vs. Contract Security

IN-HOUSE	CONTRACT
Advantages	**Advantages**
• Loyalty	• Selectivity
• Incentive	• Flexibility
• Knowledge of internal operations	• Reduction of absenteeism
• Tenure (less turnover)	• Supervision (at no cost)
• Control stays in-house	• Training (at no cost)
• Supervision stays in-house	• Objectivity
• Training geared to specific job	• Cost (20 percent less, not counting administrative costs)
• Company image improved	• Quality
• Morale	• Administration and budgeting taken care of
• Courtesy to in-house personnel	• Few union problems
• Better law enforcement liaison	• Variety of services and equipment
• Selection controlled	• Hiring and screening (at no cost)
• Better communication; more direct	• Better local enforcement contacts
	• Sharing expertise and knowledge
Disadvantages	**Disadvantages**
• Unions	• Turnover (extremely high industrywide)
• Familiarity with personnel	• Divided loyalties
• Cost	• Moonlighting (may be tired and not alert)
• Inflexibility	• Reassignment
• Administrative burdens	• Screening standards (may be inadequate)
	• Insurance

LICENSING

In-house security is generally exempt from direct provincial licensing, while all provinces license at least some categories of contract security. Saskatchewan, Ontario, and Manitoba require only that contract private investigators and security guards be licensed, but exempt all other categories. At the other end of the spectrum, British Columbia licenses private investigators, security guards, armoured car companies, locksmiths, alarm installers/ respondents, and security consultants. For details on licensing across Canada, see Table 2.1 in Chapter 2 under "Government Regulation."

The licensing of in-house security has always been a contentious issue. Most of the concerns relate to definitions and oversight. For example, would a grocery maintenance person who works after midnight also be considered a security guard of sorts? Also, if in-house security licensing were implemented, companies might start reclassifying their employees to avoid having to license them. Nova Scotia and British Columbia are the only two provinces that are actively looking for ways to license this sector. To date, the only in-house private security personnel who require licensing are those employed by permanent commercial casinos (such as those at Windsor, Rama, Niagara Falls, Hull, and Montreal). These licences are dispensed and regulated by the respective provincial gaming control commissions, rather than by private security regulators.

Since the licensing of private security personnel is in provincial jurisdiction, there are disparities from province to province. This kind of regulation will be examined more closely in Chapter 2.

GROWTH

Background

The private security industry is growing in Canada and employs more workers than the public police. That being said, attaching specific numbers with any degree of accuracy is difficult if not impossible, for the reasons provided below.

The methods by which researchers define either private security or public policing have a tremendous impact on the actual numbers. For example, excluding in-house security from the definition will greatly reduce the actual number of private security workers in Canada. Likewise, researchers will underestimate the actual number of public peace officers if they simply define them as being municipal, provincial, or federal police officers. Categories of peace officers that are typically excluded include special constables, ports police, customs and immigration officers, and fisheries officers. It is estimated that at the federal level alone, there are some forty-six departments, agencies, and Crown corporations that undertake assorted—albeit limited—law enforcement activities, such as Criminal Code enforcement and protection of property.

Another explanation for statistical discrepancies is that private security is so diverse, and that only certain segments of the industry are licensed. Many workers in the nonlicensed segment—which accounts for a large percentage of the overall industry (some estimate in-house security alone to be as much as half)—do not belong to an association, and this makes it much more difficult to find out who they are. Determining numbers even for *licensed* (and therefore supposedly registered) personnel is not always easy. For example, the security industry has a large part-time component and a traditionally high turnover rate. These two factors, combined with the fact that many provincial regulatory bodies are underresourced, make it very difficult to keep accurate data on licensed personnel.

Personnel

Very little research has been done to determine the number of people working in private security in Canada. Recent estimates indicate that this number may exceed 200 000 (Leclair et al., 1996). Besides the Leclair and Long reports, there have been two national reports that examined private security statistics regarding personnel. These were produced by the Solicitor General Canada (Normandeau and Leighton, 1990) and the Canadian Centre for Justice Statistics (Campbell and Reingold, 1994). These two reports stated that the 1990–91 figures were roughly 125 000 for private security and 55 000 for public security personnel (that is, sworn municipal, provincial, and federal officers). According to these two reports, then, the ratio of private security to public policing is slightly more than 2 to 1. Again, it is not quite clear how these figures were obtained and whether they truly represent the industry. For example, the CCJS report included certain corrections officers under the security guard classification and some quasi-police personnel (such as railway guards) under the category of private investigators. The public security personnel, on the other hand, consisted of only sworn municipal, provincial, and federal officers. Statistics Canada has not published any recent material on private security, but has updated its public policing estimate to 55 865 officers. In other words, public policing is not a major growth area.

TABLE 1.3	Number of U.S. Security Employees, 1980–2000					
Year	Contract Security Employees	Average Annual Growth Rate	In-House Security Employees	Average Annual Growth Rate	Total Private Security Employment	Total Average Annual Growth Rate
1980	556 000	n/a	420 000	n/a	976 000	n/a
1990	965 000	5.7%	528 000	2.3%	1 493 000	4.3%
1993	1 101 000	4.5%	506 100	-1.4%	1 607 000	2.5%
2000	1 473 000	4.2%	*410 000	-3.0%	1 883 000	2.3%

* The significant projected decrease in in-house security is likely due to the overall trend toward outsourcing specific services, such as security, with the objective of reducing many of the overhead costs (such as recruitment, training, benefits, and so on).

It appears that estimates of both private security and public policing are underestimated because of limited definitions of each category. However, for our purposes, we will assume that the ratio of private to public security employees is more than 3 to 1 (rather than the earlier estimates of 2 to 1).

Canada compared with U.S. and U.K.   In the United Kingdom, estimates for private security personnel vary considerably, from 130 000 to 300 000; public policing employs roughly 180 000 people (Gerden, 1995: 23). Research in the United States has been more extensive, and shows that private security employs about 1.6 million people, and public policing about 625 000. Canada's total population is 30 000 000, the United States' is 266 000 000, and United Kingdom's is 56 000 000. See Table 1.3 for U.S. Hallcrest projections on the number of employees and the growth rate.

See Figure 1.1 for Hallcrest's projection for the year 2000 on the percentage of U.S. security personnel within the overall security service and manufacturing sector.

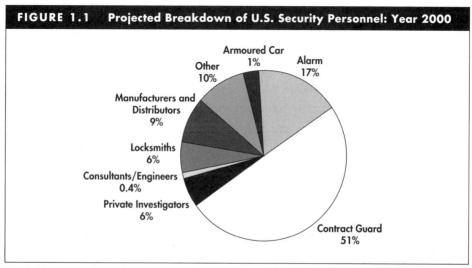

FIGURE 1.1   Projected Breakdown of U.S. Security Personnel: Year 2000

Percentages may not total 100% due to rounding.

Revenue

Very little research has been conducted into the amount of revenues generated by the Canadian private security industry. Much more research has been conducted in the United States (see Table 1.4). Determining statistics on revenues generated by the private security industry is difficult, for many of the same reasons listed earlier for personnel statistics. Leclair and Long estimate that the Canadian security industry in 1995 generated in excess of *$2.5 billion.* These authors derived these numbers from two sources: Statistics Canada and Industry Canada. Statistics Canada examined revenues from the security services component, while Industry Canada focused on security products and manufacturing. Estimated revenues in 1992 for the security services component were $1.316 billion; total revenues for the security products sector (that is, defence and industrial) were $1.3 billion.

Again, because of definitional variations, these findings are open to dispute. For example, a firm that only sells security equipment may be classified as a "retail sector" rather than "security products." It is likely that the actual revenues generated in private security are much higher than $2.5 billion. Therefore, these authors have taken a "logical leap" to peg the private security revenue figure at *$3 billion* rather than $2.5 billion. The $3 billion was also the figure estimated back in the 1990 report by the federal Solicitor General for private security revenue (Normandeau and Leighton, 1990).

The public policing sector spent approximately $5.78 billion in 1994 (Statistics Canada, 85-002). It is interesting to compare this figure to the $3 billion spent by those who used or benefited from private security services or products. Put simply, policing is a cost to all taxpayers, while private security is not.

Studies such as those conducted by Hallcrest (1992) estimated that $64 billion was spent in the United States on the private security industry. Compare this to the $35 billion that was spent in that country on public law enforcement. In other words, private security outspent public policing by 73 percent. It is predicted that by the year 2000, money spent on public policing and private security will be $44 billion and $103 billion respectively. See Table 1.4 for Hallcrest's 1993 estimates for gross annual revenues.

REASONS FOR GROWTH

Today the Canadian security industry is growing at a phenomenal rate, for several reasons, which can be broken down into the following general categories:

- Fear of crime
- Police budget cuts / Increase in certain crimes
- Increased ownership of property
- Litigation
- Insurance
- Technology
- Information security
- Privatization
- Globalization

TABLE 1.4	U.S. Security Gross Annual Revenues				
Segment	Annual Revenues and Expenditures	Average Annual Rate of Growth (since 1990)	Average Annual Rate of Growth (since 1980)	Market Share in 1990	Market Share in 1993
Armoured car	$848 000 000	4%	8%	3%	1%
Alarm companies	$6 204 400 000	11%	13%	9%	10%
Contract guard	$12 761 300 000	9%	10%	19%	20%
Private investigators	$3 065 500 000	8%	11%	5%	5%
Consultants/engineers	$478 700 000	13%	15%	1%	1%
Locksmiths	$3 673 500 000	8%	10%	6%	6%
Manufacturers and distributors	$18 960 500 000	10%	10%	28%	29%
Other	$4 456 300 000	14%	25%	6%	7%
Proprietary (in-house) security	$13 970 500 000	1%	8%	26%	22%
TOTAL	**$64 410 200 000**	**8%**	**10%**	**103%**[*]	**101%**[*]

[*] Percentages exceed 100% due to rounding.

Fear of Crime

Though crime rates are generally going down, more people are worrying today about becoming victims of crime. It follows that public security services will be pressed harder and harder to meet increased public demand. According to the General Social Survey (1993), one in four Canadians feel somewhat or very unsafe walking alone in their neighbourhood at night. This survey also indicated that fear of crime is more prevalent among females than among males, regardless of age. Despite this survey's evidence to the contrary, many people believe that the elderly are especially worried about crime. It would seem logical if they were, since they might not be able to recover from a crime as easily as those younger and usually would have more assets at stake. For the sake of accuracy, we should examine more closely the impact of crime on elderly people, since the percentage of Canadians considered elderly is increasing and this will undoubtedly influence the demand for private security services. Especially, we should keep in mind the wealth being amassed by many baby boomers, and couple this with their need for quality services (see David Foot et al., 1996).

Another probable factor here is that the media tend to increase the public's overall fear of crime. Crime reports seem to increase readership and viewership and in doing so increase media profits. For example, sensational crimes of the sort that are rarely committed—such as stranger killings—account for a large percentage of media reports. Because of how the media report crime, our perceptions of crime rates can differ from actual fact. We should remember this when reading or listening to the news, so as to maintain an appropriate perspective.

Police Budget Cuts/Increase in Certain Crimes

As governments at all levels are struggling with budgets, we are seeing a move to privatization in Canada that generally has a positive impact on private security. For example, Alberta has recently privatized the role of sheriff, thereby allowing security personnel to fill the gap. The privatization of certain policing responsibilities would also benefit private security. As police service budgets continue to shrink, police typically come to consider violent crime to be their number-one priority, and this provides an opening for other, non-police personnel to move into lesser-priority areas (such as private security). Although the overall rate of crime is stable or actually going down, the rates for many workplace or white-collar crimes, such as computer crimes, employee theft, and fraud, are increasing. Public police do not have the resources to handle these "internal" crimes. In some cases the fraud has to be in the $100 000 range for public police to give it priority. For lesser crimes, private security have to do the initial police work and, if required, hand over the file to police to initiate prosecution proceedings.

Ray (1995) points out that businesses are seeing reduced profit margins and facing potential failure because of improper or nonexistent security to protect assets. For example, one out of three small businesses fail as a result of employee theft. These thefts cost Canadian companies in excess of $20 billion a year (Foot and Stoffman, 1996: 142). Other economic crimes that are on the increase include credit card fraud, income tax evasion, telemarketing scams, and insurance fraud. According to Foot and Stoffman (1996) these increases are a result of demographics: the older criminals become, the more likely they are to move to less violent crimes such as fraud. These authors argue that age groups in society (baby boomers, baby bust, echo) do much to determine the types of crimes that will be committed.

A 1992 Angus Reid poll indicated that 58 percent "of Canadians felt that private security should assume some traditional police duties where Criminal Code offences are not involved, in order to allow police to direct more effort and personnel toward fighting serious crime." These "traditional police duties" included monitoring parking meters, controlling traffic, investigating automobile accidents, patrolling at night, responding to residential alarms, controlling crowds, providing airport and court security, and supporting police personnel. Some neighbourhoods are already hiring private security companies to conduct patrols. Ontario is presently reviewing policing services to identify core services that police must deliver and non-core functions that can be handled by other means (including private security). See Chapter 2 for more details.

Increased Ownership of Property

In the view of many, the growth of private security personnel corresponds with the increased ownership by corporations and citizens of mass private property (for example, malls and recreational areas), which is often accessible by the public. This results in a certain level of protection being demanded by the owners for these properties (Shearing and Stenning, 1983). The public police cannot always provide sufficient protection for private property, not only because of limited budgets but also because their legal authority is limited (that is, they must usually seek permission to enter private property). Also, the older people become, the more valuable and numerous their assets; their need for security rises as a result. Clearly, demographics is a factor here as well.

Litigation

Society is becoming more litigious, and private security is playing a greater role in limiting the related civil liabilities. For example, if someone trips and falls outside a retail store, security should document all factors with photographs, witness statements, and so on, to ensure the best possible defence should the case go to court. This is especially essential if the customers are Americans, who typically resort to litigation. Again, this method of reducing liability fits into the expanded role of private security mentioned earlier, where reducing loss of any type is a priority.

Insurance

Insurance premiums will often decrease if security measures are undertaken. These security measures may range from alarm systems to guards. The old adage that an ounce of prevention is worth a pound of cure is applicable. Insurance companies, like many other stakeholders, are realizing the economical benefits of proactive measures to reduce loss (as opposed to reactive measures). Proactive measures, such as the installing and monitoring of alarms, have translated into savings of up to 20 percent off household premiums.

Technology

Technology in general is becoming more affordable. As a result, the public has greater access than ever before to security products, including residential alarms, closed circuit television (CCTV), access control systems, and personal carrying alarms. The use in Canada of residential alarms is expected to grow from 5 percent of homes to over 20 percent as we enter the next millennium. Also, more and more companies are replacing some of their security personnel with security hardware. One security manager for a high-tech security firm reported that their plant in Saudi Arabia is monitored in Canada. If a problem arises, the security personnel in Canada notify the proper authorities in Saudi Arabia.

Information Security

Computer systems allow people to communicate more easily and to store all sorts of information, from financial records to R&D data. Also, many organizations are allowing the general public to access information about their activities through such vehicles as the Internet. Because of this greater reliance on computers, many companies are taking steps to ensure that restricted and sensitive information does not end up in the hands of competitors or foreign governments. Thus, some companies are now encrypting and decrypting their communications.

Corporate security personnel will need high-tech computer skills, as well as financial expertise, to reduce future losses. The days when a company simply hired an ex-police officer with twenty years of traffic experience to direct its security program are numbered.

Globalization

Trade barriers are tumbling everywhere in the world. This has resulted not only in greater competition, but also in many more opportunities to expand into new markets. Industry Canada's Sector Competitiveness Task Force Estimates found that the 1992 global market for security products, excluding the ex-Soviet Union, eastern Europe, and China, was worth C$15.5 billion. This figure broke down into $7.2 billion for defence and $8.2 billion for the industrial sector. Canada accounts for 5 percent of the total world demand for security products, and 10 percent of the total world supply. In other words, Canada exports more than it imports. The task force further estimated that markets for security products will continue to grow at an average global rate of 5 percent.

As of yet, no research concerning security services in the global market has been undertaken. Presumably, like the security product sector, there are a variety of markets for security services in the new global economy.

DEFINITIONS OF SPECIFIC CATEGORIES OF SECURITY

There are no agreed-upon definitions of private security or its subcomponents. However, I will attempt to define some of the major categories of security by referencing various statutes. These categories include the following:

- Private investigators
- Security guards
- Alarm industry
- Security consultants
- Locksmiths
- Armoured-car guards

Private Investigators

Private investigators can work for contract employers or in-house. Those working for contract agencies must be licensed in every province. Because private investigators are licensed by the provinces, there are legal definitions in place. As would be expected, these definitions vary from province to province. The province that defines a private investigator in the broadest terms is Nova Scotia, in its recent *draft* legislation, "An Act To Provide For Protective Security Services." The definition of a private investigator in this act, which will apply to those working under contract or in-house, is as follows:

a person who, for hire or renewal, investigates and provides information and includes a person who;

1. searches for and provides information as to the personal character or actions of a person, or the character or kind of business or occupation of a person.
2. searches for offenders against the law.
3. searches for missing persons or property.
4. performs services in civilian clothes for a client for the general purpose of reporting to the client upon the conduct, integrity, or trust worthiness of his or her employees.
5. searches for the causes of fire, accidents and incidents.
6. conducts tests for purposes of truth verification.

Keep in mind that this definition is still in draft. There will undoubtedly be some major complications, since the proposal includes licensing in-house private investigators. Ontario's definition, which ends at point #3 of the above definition and includes only contract private investigators, is similar to that of other Canadian provinces. It is estimated that in Canada, licensed private investigators account for about 7100 people in the private security industry (Leclair and Long, 1996).

Typical clients for private investigators include insurance companies, lawyers, corporations, and individuals. Some of the main services provided by investigators may include the following:

> risk analysis; executive background profiles; sales persons' activities; trademark, copyright, and patent infringement; conflicts of interest; corporate intelligence; wrongful dismissal claims; information leaks; computer security; industrial espionage; counter espionage; electronic surveillance; mergers and acquisitions; counter surveillance; debugging; undercover agents; driver surveillance; pre-employment background searches; shipping irregularities; nightshift activities; medical background research; integrity analysis; employee loyalty; integrity shopping; bankruptcy investigation; transshipment surveillance; solvency reports; employee attitude/morale; inventory shrinkage; WCB claims management; personality profiles; financial profiles; accuracy tests; and honesty tests (Hawkins et al, 1996: 5–6).

Security Guard

The definition of security guard varies considerably. As with private investigators, there are both contract and in-house security guards, and it is only contract guards who are licensed. This may soon change, as evidenced by actions being taken in Nova Scotia and British Columbia. Some provincial definitions include armoured car personnel, members of the Canadian Corps of Commissionaires, and bouncers. Regardless of definitions, guards form the largest segment of the private security industry. Leclair and Long (1996) report that there are 50 000 licensed security guards in Canada. Statistics Canada, which included some nonlicensed personnel in its definition (bouncers, armoured-car guards, commissionaires, correctional guards, and so on) estimated that in 1994 there were 105 000 guards. Nova Scotia's draft definition of a security guard (referred to as a "protective security officer") also includes in-house security guards. This definition consists of the following:

> a person employed by an agency for hire:
>
> 1. provides security patrols or control access to public buildings, work sites or residences during business hours or non business hours.
> 2. accompanies a guard dog while the dog is guarding or patrolling; or
> 3. provides the service of detecting theft from business namely retail security.
> 4. provides security as an armed guard as an employee of an armoured car agency.

However, a more typical definition for a security guard, as found in Ontario, is as follows:

> a person who, for hire or reward, guards or patrols for the purpose of protecting persons or property (PISGA, R.S.O., 1990 s.1).

Alarm Industry

The alarm industry is only one component of the much larger security hardware industry (see list of security products). Overall, the hardware side is reported to be growing more rapidly than any other sector in the private security industry. The alarm industry comprises firms that install, monitor, respond to, manufacture, distribute, and supply electronic alarms. The residential market for alarm systems is expected to grow rapidly in the near future. Estimates are that by the year 2000 more than 25 percent of homes will be equipped with these devices. Unfortunately, there are no accurate statistics for those employed in this field.

At present, three Canadian provinces license alarm industry personnel: British Columbia, Alberta, and Newfoundland. (Nova Scotia has legislation pending approval.) Several other provinces are now determining whether regulation of the alarm industry is required. B.C., through its Private Investigators and Security Agencies Act, defines alarm service as follows:

a person

(a) sells, supplies, provides, installs or offers to install security alarms, or

(b) repairs, maintains, monitors or responds to security alarms that are installed on the property of another,

but no person is an alarm service or carries on an alarm service by reason only that

(c) he sells, supplies or provides a security alarm, if he does not, as part of the transaction, visit or inspect the premises on which the security alarm is or has been or is to be installed, or

(d) he monitors a security alarm installed on the property of another, if he

(i) does so for no fee or other consideration, and

(ii) is not otherwise required to be licensed under this Act

The B.C. Act further defines a security alarm system so as to include "a system of security alarms and the interconnecting parts of the system [but not] a fire alarm or smoke detector." B.C. is the only province that requires alarm personnel to be trade qualified; this may require personnel to work under supervision for four years. In other words, there is a minimum standard in place for alarm personnel in B.C.

Security Consultants

This category is not well defined—it seems that almost anyone can call themselves a security consultant. Presently, only three provinces (B.C., Newfoundland, and New Brunswick) even license both security consultant firms and employees. Nova Scotia has a draft definition that includes the following:

a person who provides

1. consultation and advice on methods of protecting property from vandalism, intrusion, trespass or theft and persons from assault and theft.

2. the services of detecting electromagnetic, acoustical or other devices by which private communication or records may be intercepted, transmitted or examined.

3. audits, or designs protection programs and services including their associated management and control systems.

The difficulty in defining this category lies in the fact that many consultants are hired as business consultants, who then touch on security issues in the course of their other work. A consultant has been defined as someone who "recommends appropriate and cost-effective strategies to achieve a wide variety of security objectives, loss control, crime prevention, and investigation goals" (Sennewald, 1996: 1). It is believed that many licensed investigators and guards perform this service in the course of their regular duties.

Locksmiths

At present, locksmiths are only directly licensed in British Columbia. To some extent, the Criminal Code controls the tools used by locksmiths by creating offences for those carrying break-in instruments without lawful excuse. Also, Saskatchewan and Alberta designate this area as a trade and so have apprenticeship programs. Leclair and Long (1996) estimate that there are 2200 contract locksmiths in Canada. B.C.'s definition of a locksmith is as follows:

> a person who,
>
> 1. makes, services, repairs, codes or recodes locks,
> 2. cuts, makes, sells or otherwise provides keys from numerical or alphabetical codes or both,
> 3. sells, services or repairs safes, vaults or strongboxes, other than common strongboxes
> 4. is a member of a class of person as designated by the Lieutenant Governor in Council,
>
> but a person is not a locksmith by reason only that he
>
> - codes or recodes locks of which he is the owner, or that he has sold, or
> - cuts, makes, sells or otherwise provides a key from a numerical or alphabetical code or both, if the key is intended for use with a lock he has sold and the key is sold or provided to the owner of the lock.

Armoured-car Guards

Just over half of Canada's provinces directly license armoured-car guards. This industry exists mainly to transport cash. Some armoured-car companies also provide protection for technicians working on automated teller machines; indeed, some guards are now qualified to repair these machines themselves. There are no statistics as to the number of armoured guards in Canada. Nova Scotia's draft act refers to this category as an "armed guard," and defines it as follows:

> - a person employed in the principal activity of handling and transportation of cash, negotiable instruments or other valuable goods, who is permitted to carry a firearm under the Criminal Code for purposes of that employment.

One can only wonder whether this particular segment of the security industry will grow very much as we move toward a cashless society with its emphasis on the use of plastic cards, such as debit and credit cards.

SUMMARY

This chapter was intended to provide readers with a deeper understanding of the size and complexity of the private security industry in Canada. There are many variations and inconsistencies in this industry, many of them relating to definitions and the degree of regulation in different jurisdictions. The only clear certainty is that private security is here to stay. By all indicators, the industry will continue to grow in the next millennium, and to provide opportunities for challenging employment in Canada. Private security practitioners will require skills in communication (oral and written), and knowledge of the law and of security procedures, and also business and computer skills. Security is about reducing loss of any kind to the employer. For those who acquire the right skills to prosper in this growth industry, whether it be in the services or the products sector, the future will be exciting.

REVIEW QUESTIONS

1. Why is it difficult to specifically define private security?
2. List examples of security services and products.
3. What is the difference between in-house and contract security? Explain advantages and disadvantages of each category.
4. Explain why statistics regarding private security may be misleading.
5. What are the recent estimates concerning private security personnel and revenue in Canada and the United States?
6. Explain why private security is a growth industry.

C h a p t e r

2

ISSUES AND CHALLENGES

CHAPTER OBJECTIVES

- Recognize the complexity and diversity of the private security industry.
- Analyze specific issues and challenges being faced by the private security industry.
- Examine alternatives to present practices.

Because of unprecedented growth in the private security industry, many issues and challenges are arising that need, at the very least, to be acknowledged. In Canada, these issues can be grouped under the following headings:

- Regulation
- Training
- Wealthy versus poor
- Information protection
- Police/security overlap
- Wages
- Private justice

REGULATION

When we address the need to improve the quality of private security services and products in Canada, we must perceive the issues of regulation, standards, and training as inextricably linked. *Regulation* involves controlling private security according to certain rules; this means there must be government regulation and/or self-regulation. Similarly, *standards* involves establishing criteria for measuring quality. *Training* involves increasing the proficiency of security personnel through systematic instruction. The term *standards* is a rather generic term that can apply to many areas of the private security industry, namely, *regulation* and *training*. Therefore, instead of having a separate section on standards, I will touch on this subject throughout the chapter.

Regulation and training are two of the most discussed issues in the security industry as a whole. To a degree, most other issues in the industry tend to revolve around these two. In the past, across the country both regulation and training have been described as a "patchwork."

Government Regulation

Government or statutory regulation refers to the provincial government (which has jurisdiction over this industry as delineated by our Constitution) developing some type of mandatory licensing or regulatory scheme. All provinces have set in place some form of regulation through specific private security acts. For example, in Ontario the legislation is referred to as the Private Investigators and Security Guards Act. Similarly, most European countries and many American states have some type of government regulation (Gerden, 1995). However, ten American states still do not have any private security regulation whatsoever.

Under the various pieces of provincial legislation that require the licensing of certain categories of security, the usual practice is that both the employee and the employer (that is, the agency) must be licensed. Standards are minimal. Licensing is generally concerned with the following: criminal convictions, moral character, financial position, competency, and bondability. Usually, other conditions must also be met when establishing an agency, such as minimum insurance coverage and experience levels. All provinces require the licensing of contract security guards and private investigators. Aside from this, there are many differences between provinces in how they regulate security positions. From a government regulation perspective, British Columbia has taken the most proactive stance in Canada, in that it has required licensing for the most categories of private security, including security guards, private investigators, alarm service personnel, locksmiths, armoured-car personnel, and security consultants. In addition, B.C. is currently examining ways to license in-house security consultants. Nova Scotia is now in the process of passing new private-security legislation that would require licensing comparable to that of B.C. See Table 2.1 for types of security positions licensed in Canada.

Since certain aspects of public policing and private security are very similar (example: both are concerned with crime prevention), some proponents of government regulation often point to the various levels of formal regulation within policing as, perhaps, a justification for strengthening the accountability legislation for the private security sector. In Ontario, for example, formal accountability mechanisms in policing include the Police Services Act, the Ontario Civilian Commission on Police Services, the Special Investigations Unit, and Royal Inquiries, as well as internal affairs departments. Proponents would also argue that the industry is so diverse and competitive that it cannot regulate itself without government intervention. Opponents may answer that government regulation is too bureaucratic and that licensing is simply a revenue-generating mechanism for government.

TABLE 2.1	Government Regulated Positions Requiring Licensing

Positions	Yukon	B.C.	Alb.	Sask.	Man.	Ont.	Que.	N.B.	N.S.	P.E.I.	Nfld.
Private investigator	X	X	X	X	X	X	X	X	X	X	X
Security guard	X	X	X	X	X	X	X	X	X	X	
Armoured-car personnel	X	X*						X	X	X	X
Locksmiths		X	X**						P		
Alarm install./ respond.	X	X							P		X
Security consultants	X	X							P		X
Canadian Corps of Commissionaires							X		P		
In-house security		P							P		

X – Licensed categories

P – Proposed licensing

* – Only employers, not employees

** – Regulated by another government department aside from private security field

Self-regulation

Self-regulation involves industry members establishing standards for themselves. In Canada, for example, certain segments of the security industry voluntarily belong to associations promoting professional standards, such as the following:

- Association of Certified Fraud Examiners (ACFE)
- Canadian General Standards Board (CGSB)
- The Canadian Society for Industrial Security (CSIS)
- The American Society for Industrial Security (ASIS)
- The Federal Association of Security Officials (FASO)
- The Canadian Alarm and Security Association (CANASA)
- The International Foundation for Protection Officers (IFPO)

The private security industry in the United Kingdom is, despite recent government forays, largely self-regulated through several large associations. These include the British Security Industry Association (BSIA) and the International Professional Security Association (IPSA).

These associations in general try to "establish and maintain minimum standards for … members with respect to recruitment, training, and employment of personnel, and the quality, advertising, and selling of security products and services" (Shearing and Stenning, 1982: 48). Opponents of self-regulation point to several problems associated with this kind of control. The diversity of the security industry, in which competition is paramount, is considered a major stumbling block for getting all industries together to seek solutions. As well, self-regulated approaches typically have voluntary participation, with the result that many security firms—especially the smaller ones—do not seek membership. Another weakness is that the association members, who are nonpolice personnel, are unable to obtain criminal background checks of their members. Lastly, and perhaps most importantly, there is an actual or perceived conflict of interest when industry members establish standards and then later investigate themselves to ensure compliance.

On the other hand, self-regulation would allow the industry owners, much like any other business owners throughout the country, to determine for themselves how to run their businesses. This would reduce government red tape (many believe that governments are too far removed from the process and/or too political to make competent decisions concerning the regulation of the industry). Some argue that the licensing requirements of contract security companies are already too heavily regulated relative to other private enterprises.

Combination

A combination strategy involves mixing government regulation with self-regulation. Opponents of government regulation assert that a better solution for setting standards would be a stakeholder approach involving the security industry, government, police, security clients, the general public, and academics. The bringing together of key stakeholders to improve standards for security guards in Canada has been examined by the Canadian General Standards Board (CGSB). The thinking behind this board's approach is that the clients will demand that security guard companies follow the standards set forth by the CGSB.

Advisory boards, consisting of representative stakeholders who advise the registrar, are another form of combination strategy. The advice given may involve policies, procedures, standards, codes of ethics, and training. These boards could be involved in fact finding and make nonbinding recommendations concerning disciplinary problems of licensees. The B.C. Commission of Inquiry into Policing stated the importance of establishing board guidelines relating to the following: representation of industry, minimum qualifications of board members, membership length, formal and informal mechanisms for industry consultation, and reporting requirements.

Other Forms of Governance

Regulatory practices aside, the private security industry is influenced by a number of factors including clients, unions, owners, customers of organizations, and marketplace dynamics, as well as by a number of "indirect" laws. In particular, the client has a lot of control over the contract security industry. For example, the client can demand that the security meet minimum standards. If the contract company does not perform well enough, remedies open to the client range from not renewing the contract to terminating the contract before completion and possibly seeking damages. An example pertaining to the power of the owner involves recruitment of security personnel. It is obviously in the owner's best interest to seek qualified people, and therefore there is a large onus to hire the "right" people, as opposed to relying on others (such as government) to determine competency or reliability.

Some of the "indirect" laws referred to earlier include the Criminal Code, tort law, property law, contract law, employment and labour relations law, and human rights law, as well as the Charter of Rights and Freedoms. For example, as a general rule the Criminal Code allows private security agents the same authority to arrest and detain as any private individual. Likewise, the use of force is governed by both criminal and civil laws. Thus, security agents who use excessive force may be subject to both criminal and civil liability. The criminal charge may be for assault; civilly, they may be held responsible for torts such as assault, false imprisonment, and/or malicious prosecution. See Chapter 3 for more details.

So even if no formal regulation exists, there are still many factors that place controls on security personnel and companies. However, many of the above measures are typically more reactive than proactive. Being sued after the fact rather than preventing the occurrence in the first place is a typical example of a reactive measure.

TRAINING

Training goes hand in hand with regulations, be they government or otherwise. Once the type of regulation is established, then training is probably the next big issue. To date, only British Columbia and Newfoundland have mandatory training for certain kinds of security positions. As a whole, British Columbia's training is far more extensive than Newfoundland's one-time correspondence course. B.C. already has minimum training for security guards and minimum qualifications in the alarm industry; that province is also looking at ways to establish training requirements for private investigators, armoured-car personnel, locksmiths, security consultants, and possibly the in-house security sector. In Newfoundland, on the other hand, private investigators and security guards need only complete a one-time correspondence course or take an equivalent course at an approved educational facility. As mentioned earlier, Nova Scotia is in the early stages of establishing minimum training standards.

As a general rule, however, there are no minimum training requirements in the security industry, and this makes for tremendous variations in standards from one company to the next. I have heard of Ontario companies that hired, licensed, and assigned guard duties to individuals on the same day, even though those people had no training or previous security experience.

The contract guard industry is highly competitive and the lowest bid often gets the contract. Quite often, to offer the lowest bid, a company will greatly reduce if not entirely eliminate expenses such as training. Most positions in security require at least some training in areas such as legal powers, communication (oral and written), and procedures. For example, even if a guard is told not to make arrests, he or she should still be aware of the legal limits.

Studies have indicated that the larger the company, the more likely it is to invest in training. Smaller companies have fewer resources to do so. Such a disparity in training can only exist where there is no mandatory training requirement. In 1993, Bonnie Erickson of the University of Toronto completed a study of the contract security industry in Toronto. She found that 26 percent of security employees (guards, investigators, alarm personnel) and 24 percent of security supervisors stated that they received no training from their companies. Almost half of the employees and supervisors who received training stated that it consisted of, at most, one day. In addition, 48 percent of employees and 51 percent of supervisors reported that their training was adequate.

Erickson also found that security personnel (all levels) typically have about fourteen years of schooling. Between 80 and 90 percent have a high school degree, and many of them have some postsecondary schooling. Statistics Canada (Juristat, 1994) noted in 1991 that investigators and guards had the levels of education indicated in Table 2.2.

TABLE 2.2 1991 Education Levels: Investigators and Guards	
Education	**Percentage**
University degree	6%
Some university	39%
Trade diploma	4%
High school diploma	18%
Grade 9–13	23%
Less than grade 9	10%

Leclair and Long (1996) surveyed readers of *Canadian Security Magazine*, most of whom are security managers, and found the levels of education reported in Table 2.3.

TABLE 2.3 Canadian Security Magazine Survey	
Education	**Percentage**
Postgraduate degree	3%
Bachelor degree	11%
College diploma	25%
Some college or university	32%
High school diploma	25%
No high school diploma	2.4%

Percentages may not total 100, due to rounding.

Another study, which examined the contract security industry in Ontario in the late 1970s, found that "contract security persons receive very little formal training" (Shearing et al., 1980: 135). This same study reported that many security personnel felt that their training was inadequate. Also, many studies that have examined training have found discrepancies between employers and employees regarding what each said about the amount and type of training provided by companies.

In regard to specific legal knowledge, Erickson's Toronto study found that security employees and supervisors were less informed than managers and owners about what constituted a criminal offence (see Table 2.4). As well, Erickson found that security guards were least knowledgeable about the law, and that private investigators were the most knowledgeable. Shearing and Stenning (1980) found similar results in their 1970s study of the contract security industry: they determined that many security personnel did not know the law as it applied to them or the public.

In another security opinion poll, 58 percent of Canadians, 40 percent of lawyers, and 24 percent of police felt that private security should assume some traditional police duties in order that the police could focus on serious crime fighting (Chapman Report, 1992: 2). This report also indicated that over half of those who opposed private security involvement cited inadequate training as their main reason for opposition. Thus, one can logically assume that training will be a key issue as the private security industry continues to grow.

TABLE 2.4   Percentage of Security Personnel Who Say That an Act is Classified as a Criminal Offence

Act	Employee	Supervisor	Manager	Owner	Guard	Investigator	Alarm Worker	Don't Know
Possession of weapon	99	100	100	99	98	100	99	1
Setting fire to company property	99	98	100	99	99	99	100	1
Assisting person to escape	97	98	100	100	99	97	100	1
Theft of company property (>$1000)	99	93	97	99	97	97	99	1
Possession of narcotic	97	98	97	97	99	97	100	1
Assaulting a company employee	98	96	96	95	96	99	98	2
Destroying company property	86	84	88	87	86	88	88	6
Theft (<$1000)	82	80	84	85	76	89	91	3
Setting false fire alarm	81	85	85	86	83	90	87	9
Creating a disturbance	49	67	61	62	47	73	55	6
Trespassing on company property	57	59	49	47	55	55	55	7
Picketing illegally	48	51	35	37	45	40	49	16
Being drunk on company property	31	22	20	17	26	18	30	8
Drinking on company property	37	26	15	7	30	6	27	6
Insulting a security officer	18	12	7	10	16	9	15	8
Parking on company property	16	7	0	6	21	6	7	7

The B.C. Commission of Inquiry gave the following reasons why the training of security guards is important:

- The physical and economic security of businesses and their employees.
- The need to guarantee civil liberties and public safety.
- The increasing use of private security by public institutions.
- The poor image of security personnel, which can discourage public and police support for their activities.

This commission then provided the following recommendations concerning the training of security guards:

- Require specific training standards for all security guard/patrol personnel and their supervisors.
- Require all security guards/personnel to attain these standards within a specified period of time.
- Ensure that training programs are based on the principles of comprehensiveness, accessibility, affordability, flexibility, and consistency.
- Establish periodic retraining of private security personnel.
- Establish periodic review and revision of training standards.

Private investigators, who have significant potential to invade the privacy of individuals, require training as well. The commission noted that training for private investigators should include course work, examinations, and apprenticeship periods. With regard to the latter, the apprenticeship program must be clear with respect to what should be done, and who should supervise, as well as the need for precise reporting requirements.

Moylan and Pitre (1996) conducted a national survey of training and education issues facing the Canadian security sector, and made the following observations:

- The professional relationship between the security industry and the providers of security training and education is weak at best.
- Training and education programs are operating in a void, with no relationship between institutions and industry.
- Very few graduates receive certification from national organizations upon graduation from their respective programs.
- There is little provincial legislation addressing the issues of training of security personnel, their certification, and program accreditation.
- There is little recent scholarly research addressing issues relating to security.
- There is an absence of security-related programs at the university level.
- There is no Canadian resource centre/clearing house on security matters.
- The RCMP and similar government organizations could be important security training resources.

WEALTHY VERSUS POOR

The unprecedented growth in private security raises some crucial questions about who in society is able to have this extra protection. This question is particularly important in light of the dwindling resources in the public sector. The "rule of law" in Canada allows everyone the right to equal protection; even so, the following questions need to be addressed: Will private security ultimately be seen as something only the rich can afford? Will we end up with different levels of policing depending on ability to pay? Can protection based on income even be justified, in that there already exists much disparity in many other areas of life between the haves and the have-nots?

Even now, the more affluent members of society can afford better protection than the poor, in that they can afford to buy alarms for their cars and homes. Also, we are beginning to see the well-to-do moving into neighbourhoods that are virtually gated communities. Some of these communities have gone to the extent of hiring private security to control such things as entrance and exit points, and installing barbwire fencing. California alone has over 500 000 "fortress" communities.

The trend toward gated communities such as townhouse complexes is likely to continue as the baby boomers move into their 50s. A substantial number of people are entering their retirement years, many of them "boomers" holding significant wealth. This, and the growing fear of crime, provides the right climate for this trend to perpetuate itself.

Is Canada becoming a society in which those who cannot afford private security must rely on the public policing system for their security needs? It is important to note that despite some drawbacks, private security has many benefits, such as the ability at times to respond better to client needs. For example, private security often takes a more proactive approach to problems, as opposed to the more traditional reactive approach applied by many police services.

INFORMATION PROTECTION

What methods will private security firms use to obtain information? What will they do with this information once they have obtained it? These privacy concerns need to be examined, especially in light of police and security exchanging information, and foreign ownership of security companies. Such concerns will no doubt increase, since we now live in an information-based society in which information is easily accessed by computer.

A number of provinces have laws that touch on this concern. For example, in Ontario the Private Investigators and Security Guards Act has its section 24, which states that "no person shall divulge to anyone, except as is legally required, any information acquired by him or her as a private investigator." However, this does little to address the following questions:

- Who is legally required to know?
- What controls are in place for those private security personnel who are not licensed private investigators?
- Can section 24 be interpreted to mean that anyone who pays the investigator to seek information can be considered "legally required"?
- What controls are in place once the client receives this newly found information?

Another privacy issue is how much "confidential" information is passed between public and private security personnel. This transferring of information is often facilitated by the movement of public police to private security (Shearing et al., 1980: 195). Research published in the late 1970s and early 1980s found that 38 percent of contract security executives interviewed (Shearing et al., 1980: 118) and 32 percent of in-house executives (Jeffries, 1977: 38) were former police officers. There is anecdotal evidence that more and more private security personnel are being recruited from nonpolicing backgrounds; even so, the movement of police to private security will undoubtedly gather momentum as more higher-ranking police officers retire, especially in light of the trend toward decentralization whereby authority is pushed further toward the front-line personnel (that is, the constables).

Despite various pieces of legislation that prohibit it (including police services acts and freedom of information and protection of privacy acts), the passing of confidential information to private security from government sources is still a common practice. This is evident in the following excerpt from Shearing and Stenning (1983: 503). The researchers interviewed a private investigator about information exchanged between him and various public agencies:

> There are approximately a hundred private investigators in Toronto who can literally get any information they want whether it is from the Police Department, Workmen's Compensation records, O.H.I.P. [Ontario Health Insurance Plan], insurance records, or whatever. In the space of a ten-minute telephone conversation I can get what it would take me perhaps three weeks to discover. With experience and contacts, a well-established investigator can provide a better quality of information and can do so at a much lower cost to his client even though his hourly rates might be twice as much as a new investigator might charge.

Police often seek information from those in private business, especially those in security positions. This practice of give-and-take allows the police to "end run" the judicial process— for example, by circumventing or at least delaying the need for a warrant for information. Information gathered in this way is probably not admissible in court but can still be very useful to a police investigation. Where information is concerned, the ends are often seen as justifying the means.

Are there proper controls in place to ensure that foreign executives are held accountable for the actions of their security personnel working in Canada? In a 1976 study, Shearing and colleagues found that 20 percent of the private-security agencies operating in Ontario were foreign (American) owned, and that these employed 43 percent of total licensed security agents. There has been no systematic research in this area since this 1976 study. Besides the American firms, Group 4 (British) and Barnes Security (Australian) also have Canadian branches.

In 1980 the Krever Commission examined the confidentiality of health information. American executives of security companies operating in Canada were requested by Justice Krever to appear. These executives failed to appear because they were beyond the jurisdiction of the commission (Shearing et al., 1982). The following questions, as developed by Shearing and colleagues (1980), are still relevant and need to be addressed:

- Are the activities of Canadian subsidiaries directly controlled by their American parent companies?

- Will large, foreign-owned companies ultimately monopolize the industry in Canada because of subsidies that allow them to underbid for contracts and provide better-qualified personnel?
- Does confidential information leave Canada along with large amounts of Canadian capital?
- Do we have enough information to accurately assess the degree of foreign participation in the Canadian security industry?
- Does foreign control of contract security pose a threat to Canadian sovereignty?

For an indication as to how much money is at stake involving foreign countries, Cunningham and colleagues (1990) estimated that in the United States between 1985 and 1989, British, Swiss, Australian, and Japanese companies invested $4 billion in American security companies.

POLICE/SECURITY OVERLAP

The line between public police and private security is becoming blurred. For example, many off-duty police officers are being hired to protect private property—for example, at concerts and sporting events. *The Globe and Mail* reported that in 1992 the Metropolitan Toronto Police received almost $9 million on top of salaries from providing services to private clients. It is reported that in the United States, some police officers make more money working off-duty for private clients than on-duty working for the public. There are important issues here that must be addressed, such as whether off-duty police amount to unfair competition for nonpolice security personnel, and whether a conflict of interest exists when a public police officer is being directed by someone whose main (if not only) concern is profits rather than due process.

Conversely, private security personnel are being hired more than ever before to protect the types of private property to which the public is allowed access—that is, bars, shopping malls, entertainment areas, and the like. Private security is also making inroads into what traditionally was a police domain. For example, Norman Inkster, former commissioner of the RCMP, reported in a 1994 speech in Hong Kong that a fraud will soon have to be in the $100 000 range before police will be required to investigate. In other words, the private sector—namely, private security—will have to investigate many such crimes, and if a prosecution is sought, private security will have to provide all the background information to the police and the Crown.

Ontario's Solicitor General is presently reviewing many issues associated with policing, including the financing of police services; the structure and organization of police services; policing functions; and the civilian governance of police services. Undoubtedly, by the end of this process private security will be permitted to assume more responsibility in areas once considered the exclusive domain of public police services.

In a 1996 discussion paper on policing services in Ontario, the categories listed below were designated as core policing functions and ancillary tasks. For the core functions there will be no sweeping transfer of responsibilities to private security. However, the private sector—particularly private security—is likely to become a more active partner in the ancillary tasks.

Core functions

- Crime prevention
- Law enforcement, including apprehending criminals, laying charges, and participating in prosecutions
- Assistance to victims of crime
- Public order maintenance activities, including activities designed to prevent breaches of the peace
- Emergency response

Ancillary functions

- Care and control of prisoners
- Prisoner transportation
- Court security
- The issuance of summonses
- Other types of activities that are currently provided by police services

The same discussion paper lists various options to be considered for delivering certain policing functions, including the use of civilians, special constables, unpaid volunteers, auxiliaries, other personnel (municipal, private, and nonprofit), and public/private partnerships. Note well that this paper further states that before any of the above options are considered, issues related to selection, training, equipment, uniforms, accountability, and liability will have to be addressed.

In mid-January 1997, Ontario's Solicitor General presented a follow-up to its 1996 discussion paper. Unfortunately, this more recent document did not elaborate on the issue of devolving certain responsibilities to nonpolice personnel (that is, to private security). The document did, however, shed some light on changes regarding budgets, financing, police services boards, and oversight mechanisms. It also stressed the same core police functions.

In light of these reviews in Ontario, and others throughout Canada, an examination of opinion polls on the future of private security is warranted. An Angus Reid study for the Canadian Society of Industrial Security reported in 1992 (p. 2) that 58 percent of Canadians believed "that private security should assume some traditional police duties where Criminal Code offences are not involved, in order to allow police to direct more effort and personnel toward serious crime." The same study listed the categories of duties where private security could be involved, along with the corresponding rate of support from the Canadian public (Table 2.5).

A 1981 Hallcrest survey found that in the United States, many law enforcement executives believed that private security could perform more cost-effectively than police in certain activities, including the following: "public building security, parking enforcement, parking lot patrol, school crossing guards, public parks patrol, animal control, traffic control, non-injury accident investigation, special events security, city/county code violations, funeral escorts, court security, prisoner transport, and housing project patrol" (Cunningham et al, 1990: 272).

TABLE 2.5	Percentage of Canadians polled who strongly/moderately agree with private security involvement in selected duty areas.
Monitoring parking meters and issuing tickets for illegal parking	78%
Traffic control and highway speed patrol	43%
Automobile accident investigations	42%
Night-time security patrols	65%
Responding to residential alarms	49%
Airport security	67%
Supporting police personnel in by-law enforcement	73%
Crowd control	54%
Court security	60%

WAGES

Recently, there have been three somewhat incomplete studies of wages in the private security industry. In one of these studies Statistics Canada, using 1991 Census data, looked at the wages of public police, private investigators, and security guards across Canada (Juristat, 1994). The definitions used by this study for private investigators and security guards included both contract and in-house sectors. The second study was conducted by Bonnie Erickson (1993), who examined 1991 data for the contract security industry in Toronto. Lastly, in 1995 Leclair and Long (1996) conducted a survey of the security industry using readers of *Canadian Security Magazine* as a sample. Most of the respondents in this last study were security managers.

Statistics Canada found that in 1991, on a national average, private investigators earned $33 500 and guards earned $21 263. Similarly, Erickson's study found that guards in Toronto shared a median salary between $20 000 and $24 999, while investigators' and hardware workers' median salaries were $35 000 to $44 999. Erickson also reported median salaries for the following categories of contract security personnel: employees and supervisors, $25 000 to $34 999; managers, $45 000 to $54 999; owners, $55 000 to $64 999. Leclair and Long found that guards were generally in the $17 000 to $22 000 range. They added that in 1995, 38 percent of security managers indicated that they would earn more than $55 000 for that year. Interestingly, the American Hallcrest report estimated that the wage for in-house and contract unarmed guards was $7.70 per hour, or approximately U.S. $16 000 annually for a 40-hour week.

PRIVATE JUSTICE

There are two kinds of justice: **public** and **private**. *Public* justice—specifically criminal justice—involves the police and Crown; it is concerned with due process and treats the state as the victim. In a corporate setting, *private* justice is concerned mainly with ways to reduce loss, thereby maximizing profits. Each type of justice needs to be examined further with the goal of deciding on the optimal route.

Example: Consider a case of employee theft from an industrial setting. First of all, there is no law which states that the employer *must* inform the police after discovering the theft. So, the employer needs to decide whether to handle the matter internally or externally. *Internally* means invoking company policy on discipline procedures; this route may involve input from management, security, unions, and the offender. *Externally* means involving the police, followed (perhaps) by the courts, the Crown, and perhaps the corrections system.

Shearing and Stenning (1982) speak of the internal process as being much more informal than the external one. They further point out the following implications of going the "external" route:

- Losing the employee's services, temporarily or permanently
- Temporary loss of property while it is being used as evidence
- Expense and use of personnel in assisting police investigation and testifying before court
- Potential negative effect on employee morale
- Union intervention that could potentially lead to a strike in support of the employee

One should also be concerned with the fact that the burden of proof in a criminal case is "beyond a reasonable doubt," which can be a difficult threshold to reach. And if the employee is fired, and later acquitted in a criminal trial, there may be some civil action open to the employee, such as a wrongful dismissal suit. In other words, an employee fired for theft may well sue if found not guilty.

On the other hand, if the internal process is selected, it is "likely to be resolved through negotiation, mediation and settlement, than through any formal adjudicative process" (Shearing and Stenning, 1982: 35). As well, the underlying theme of this approach is not punishing the employee, but rather preventing this kind of loss to the company in the future (that is, on establishing new policy).

There are problems associated with private justice, even when a union is involved. Some of these relate to the lack of legal rights accorded to the employee—rights that are closely associated with the more formal criminal justice system. Potential abuses in private justice include searching employees without consent or by intimidation, and forcing them to incriminate themselves. Note that private security personnel are not restrained by the Charter of Rights and Freedoms the way public officers are, since the former typically do not perform a governmental function. I will examine these legal concerns in the next chapter. Other ethical problems associated with private justice include the fact that most decisions are based on economics—namely, the best way to increase profits—instead of due process, and that certain rights and privileges may be lost along the way. In fact, private justice can often mete out a more severe penalty than the courts; consider that the penalties under this system may include loss of employment, loss of pension and benefits, and sufficient damage to the employee's reputation that future work in a similar field may be difficult to find.

Still, there are advantages and disadvantages to both types of justice. Even when both parties—the employee who got caught stealing, and the employer—would rather deal with the issue internally, one must be aware of the greater potential for an abuse of rights.

SUMMARY

This chapter presented a brief picture of some of the major issues and challenges being faced by the private security industry in Canada. These issues include the following:

- Regulation
- Training
- Wealthy versus poor
- Wages
- Police/security overlap
- Private justice

We must acknowledge and address these issues, especially in light of trends which suggest that the industry will continue to grow into the next millennium. The increased presence of private security is a reality to which we cannot turn a blind eye; nor can we ignore the challenges the industry is facing. None of the issues discussed in this chapter are insurmountable, provided that proper attention is given to the stakeholders involved.

REVIEW QUESTIONS

1. Fully explain four issues facing the security industry in Canada.
2. List and explain the different types of private security regulation.
3. Are the types of regulation mentioned in question 2 mutually exclusive? Explain.
4. Should government play a major role in the private security industry? List some advantages and disadvantages of this involvement.
5. What are the typical salaries for guards and investigators in Canada?

LEGAL

AUTHORITY

CHAPTER OBJECTIVES

- Explain the concept of criminal law.
- Define arrest and detention.
- Identify when a private citizen has the authority to perform an arrest.
- Identify when a private citizen has the authority to perform a search.
- List the steps to a citizen's arrest.
- Define civil law.
- Explain how civil law is important to those working in private security.

BACKGROUND

There are essentially two classes of laws in Canada: public and private. *Public* law is concerned mainly with relationships between individuals (including organizations) and government. *Private* law, also referred to as *civil* law (not to be confused with Quebec's Civil Code, discussed below) is concerned mainly with relationships between individuals or

TABLE 3.1 Division of Public/Private Law	
Public Law	**Private (Civil) Law**
• **criminal**	• **contract**
• constitutional	• **tort**
• administrative	• property
• military	• family
• international	• trust, patent, copyright

organizations. This type of law typically, but not always, involves lawsuits in which one party is seeking compensation. Both classes of laws have a significant bearing on the actions of security personnel.

Public and private law can be further divided into the categories listed in Table 3.1. The highlighted areas will be discussed in greater detail later in this chapter.

There are also regulatory offences, which can result in imprisonment or fines; these are neither public nor civil, but somewhere in between. Regulatory offences of concern to private security include many provincial laws such as, in Ontario, the Private Investigator and Security Guards Act (PISGA), the Trespass to Property Act (TPA), the Liquor License Act (LLA), and the Highway Traffic Act (HTA). Regulatory offences are part of a "grey area" but are generally considered civil laws. The rest of this chapter will focus on criminal, contract, and tort law and on the regulatory offences mentioned earlier. But for the sake of context, before we delve into these specific areas of law we will briefly examine some history of law.

HISTORY OF LAW

Common and Civil Law

Essentially, Canada was created by the British North America Act, 1867 (now referred to as the Constitution Act, 1867). Many laws have been created (and often changed) in the 130 years since Confederation. However, laws have always existed in human society, and it is worth discussing those earlier laws that shaped (and continue to shape) Canada's present laws. In this context, the two major *systems* of law in the Western world are the common law and the civil law (not to be confused with the *class* of law known also as civil law, discussed earlier).

I will explain the two systems of law, but only briefly, since security personnel do not need an in-depth knowledge of either. The **civil law** system, which is used in many European countries, has been traced to Roman law. This system of law has been codified (that is, written down) in extensive legal texts. The civil law system was formally codified mainly during the reigns of the emperors Justinian and Napoleon: thus, the Justinian and Napoleanic Codes. These codes dealt with both public and private law.

Common law originated in England and is the system of law used in most English-speaking countries (including the United States, Canada, and Australia). This system can be traced back to the era when feudal lords heard disputes between peasants. After the Norman

Conquest in 1066, judges in England were sent out to settle disputes. Instead of relying on texts like the civil system, these judges relied on their common sense to make decisions. However, common sense is a very subjective process. As time passed, the judges became aware of their inconsistencies and began trying to follow one another's judicial decisions when the facts and circumstances were similar. Thus, the law was made more "common" to all; thus, the "common" law. Common law is also referred to as judge-made law, or case law. During the nineteenth century the practice of trying to follow previous decisions led to the formal rule of precedent (or *stare decisis*). The rule of precedent, which exists today in Canada, basically means that the courts must follow decisions of higher-level courts and should try to follow courts of equal level when the facts and circumstances are similar. For example, if the Supreme Court of Canada makes a ruling concerning the actions of private security personnel, it will affect all the courts in Canada. However, a decision by the Alberta Court of Appeal would bind the courts only in that province. Other provincial courts of appeal in this case would try to follow Alberta's decision.

Quebec, with its Civil Code, is the only province in Canada that uses the civil system of law. Even in Quebec, however, this system is used mainly in matters of private law, such as contracts, wills, and property. The other Canadian provinces use the common law as the basis for their private laws. Though the two systems are different, they are generally quite similar in substance. All ten provinces (this includes Quebec) use the common law as the basis for public laws, including the criminal law. The criminal law, as we will discuss below, is created by the federal government and so applies equally to all parts of Canada; in contrast, in the United States each state can also make criminal law. The rest of this chapter will focus on those areas of the law that are rooted in common law.

The common law almost always needs updating or modernizing. For example, there were no motor vehicles or information superhighways during the common law era; it follows that there would obviously have been no rulings in these matters. This modernization has been effected through **statutes,** which override the common law. Statutes are laws made by elected officials of government, whether provincial or federal. (Municipal laws, though similar in concept to statutes, are called by-laws.) Statutes are also referred to as legislative law or government-made law. For example, all of our criminal offences have been codified or put into statute form (thus the Criminal Code), with one exception: the offence of contempt of court is still in common law form, presumably to allow judges greater discretion. As well, many defences for crimes are still found under common law and not in statute form. Likewise, much of our private law has not been codified and is still found under common law. Before we delve into specific aspects of the law, we need to look at what level of government can make laws.

CONSTITUTION

Background

The formal "law-making law" in Canada, which determines what kinds of laws a particular level of government can enact, is the Constitution Act, 1867 (formerly known as the British North America Act, 1867). There is also the Constitution Act, 1982, which we will discuss later on. The 1867 document created a federal structure of government for Canada—that is, one with a national government to make laws for the entire country, as well as provincial governments to control provincial and local affairs. Municipal governments are given their authority at the discretion of each provincial government (thus, Prince Edward Island has no municipal governments). Table 3.2 shows which areas the Constitution has given the federal and provincial governments. The highlighted areas have particular relevance to the private security industry.

It would be wise to keep in mind that the jurisdictions listed are not precisely defined, and can be interpreted in a variety of different ways. This has resulted in much debate between the various levels of government. This blurring of the roles is found, for example, in driving laws. In Ontario's Highway Traffic Act (HTA) the offence of careless driving is not a crime. However, the Criminal Code, which is federal legislation, has a similar offence known as dangerous driving. Thus, one could argue the legitimacy of both offences, since the province is responsible for local matters (such as driving) and the federal government is responsible for criminal laws and for the peace, order, and good government of Canada (which relates to public safety issues). In theory, the same argument could be raised as to which level of government has jurisdiction over the private security industry. Currently, the provincial governments directly control this industry, since it is considered a local matter. However, could the federal government not make the same argument as above concerning the need for peace, order, and good government, since private security has the potential to significantly invade our personal privacy?

TABLE 3.2 **Breakdown of Authority by Constitution**	
Federal Powers	**Provincial Powers**
• **To make laws for the peace, order and good government of Canada**	• Direct taxation within the province for the province
• Regulation of trade and commerce	• Management and sale of public lands belonging to the province
• Unemployment insurance	• **Provincial prisons**
• Taxation	• Hospitals, asylums, charities
• Postal service	• Municipal institutions in the province
• Census and statistics	• Shops, saloons, auctions
• Military	• Solemnization of marriage
• Beacons, buoys, lighthouses	• **Property and civil rights in the province**
• Navigation and shipping	• **Administration of justice in the province, including the constitution, maintenance, and organization of provincial courts, both civil and criminal jurisdiction, including procedure in civil matters in those courts**
• Ferries between provinces	
• Currency and coinage	
• Banking, issue of paper money	
• Interest	• **Imposition of punishment by fine, penalty, or imprisonment for enforcing any law in province**
• Bankruptcy	
• Patents of invention and discovery	• **Generally, all matters of merely local or private nature in the province**
• Copyrights	
• Lands reserved for native people	• Education
• Marriage and divorce	• After 1982, each province has control over non-renewable natural resources, forestry products, and electric power
• Naturalization and aliens	
• **Criminal law (except the administration of courts)**	
• **Penitentiaries**	

When jurisdictional disputes occur, as they often do, the courts are the ultimate authority for clarification. In addition, our Constitution (that is, the Constitution Act, 1867 and 1982) is considered the **supreme law** which cannot be violated. If a government oversteps its jurisdiction—for example, if the provinces enact criminal law—the Supreme Court of Canada may find that the law has no force or effect, rendering it unenforceable, or *ultra vires*. Parliamentary supremacy refers to Parliament (federal or provincial) being supreme within its jurisdiction and having the authority to overrule all other laws—including the common law—except those laws found in the Constitution, which includes the Charter of Rights and Freedoms. Thus, if a government creates a law that has not violated the Constitution or is within its constitutional authority, that law is deemed enforceable, or *intra vires*.

Charter of Rights and Freedoms

In 1982, under Prime Minister Pierre Trudeau, two major changes to our Constitution were made in what is known as the Constitution Act, 1982. First, the Constitution was patriated or "brought home" to Canada (till then, it had been a British statute). This meant that Canada could now change the Constitution without having to seek approval from Britain. Canada was now truly independent; however, when it tried to change its Constitution by means of a new amending formula, it met with failure at the Meech Lake and Charlottetown Accords.

Second, the Constitution Act, 1982, included the Canadian Charter of Rights and Freedoms. The Charter has a special relevance to the actions of security personnel that will be discussed later. This Charter contains 34 sections that set out certain individual rights and freedoms which, with few exceptions, cannot be infringed upon by government. The Bill of Rights, created in 1960, is similar to the Charter in content but does not have the same authority, since it is only a federal statute and not placed within the Constitution. In other words, since the Charter is part of our Constitution, it is a supreme law in Canada and overrides all other government-made law. In general terms, any government law or statute that violates this Charter will be deemed unenforceable by the courts.

There are eight specific rights and freedoms protected in the Charter; these are listed below, with examples. It is important to understand from the outset that the Charter, as stated in section 32(1), only applies to governmental laws and actions (federal, provincial, municipal); in disputes between private individuals or organizations, it would only apply if one of the parties was government or if the actions undertaken by the individual or organization were seen as governmental actions. For example, when citizens make arrests their actions are considered governmental actions and therefore the legal rights section of the Charter applies. So when retail stores, acting on their own, install cameras in washrooms to deter shoplifting, the Charter's legal rights section dealing with unreasonable search and seizure (s.8) does not apply, because this is a private matter not dealing with government and not considered a government action (*R. v. Swanarchuk*, 1990). Other laws, such as human rights and privacy legislation, could possibly prohibit this type of intrusion, since it is not covered under the Charter. In simplest terms, the Charter is concerned with governmental action rather than private action. Later in this chapter we will discuss further the issue of Charter applicability in regard to security actions.

- *Fundamental Freedoms (s.2)*   Includes freedom of conscience, religion, thought, expression, peaceful assembly, association.

- *Democratic Rights (s.3–5)*   Includes the right to vote in elections and qualify for membership.

- *Mobility Rights (s.6)*   Includes the right to remain in or leave Canada, or move to any province.

- *Legal Rights (s.7–14)*   Includes (s.7) the right to life, liberty, and security of the person in accordance with fundamental justice; (s.8) the right to be free from unreasonable search and seizure; (s.9) the right not to be arbitrarily detained or imprisoned; (s.10b) the right to counsel; (s.11d) the right to be presumed innocent; (s.11b) the right to be tried within a reasonable time; and (s.12) the right be free from cruel or unusual punishment.

- *Equality Rights (s.15 and 28)*   Includes the right to equal protection and benefit of the law without being discriminated against based on race, national or ethnic origin, colour, religion, sex, age, and mental or physical disability.

- *Language Rights (s.16–22)*   Includes the right to access information from the Government of Canada in either French or English.

- *Minority Language Education Rights (s.23)*   Includes the right to learn either French or English in primary and secondary schools.

- *Native Rights (s.25)*   Provides that the Charter does not change any existing native rights that existed before its inception.

Of all the above rights, the legal rights section has the most impact on the actions of private security personnel. Specifically, we will examine sections 7 to 10 within the criminal law context. However, before we delve into this area, be aware that all our Charter rights are not absolute: certain rights may be violated in specific situations. There are two sections of the Charter that can limit our Charter rights: section 1 and section 33.

Section 1, known as the "common sense" clause, allows the violation of these rights "subject only to such reasonable limits prescribed by law as can be demonstrably justified in a free and democratic society" (s.1). This means that a law which violates the Charter will be considered "saved" under section 1 as a reasonable limit, if its objective is sufficiently important to society that overriding a constitutionally protected right is warranted. For example, during a RIDE program, when you are stopped by a police officer and asked to submit to a roadside test with an approved screening device, you are in effect being detained. Under the legal rights section, when you are detained by police you should be given your right to counsel. But in *R. v. Therens*, 1986, the courts stated that in the interest of preventing loss caused by drunk drivers, the police officer does not have to inform the driver of the right to counsel, with few exceptions (such as excessive delays), since that would prevent the police from checking a large number of people at any given time. The courts further stated that in this particular situation, the Charter violation was reasonable, and therefore saved under section 1. Besides the right to counsel, other rights violated during a RIDE program include sections 7 and 9.

Section 1 has also been successfully invoked in matters relating to mandatory retirement ages (equality rights), random stopping of vehicles under the HTA (legal rights), defamation of character laws (fundamental freedoms), and border searches (legal rights).

Section 33 of the Charter, known as the notwithstanding clause, allows government to basically ignore section 2 (fundamental freedoms) and sections 7 to 15 (legal and equality rights) at their discretion. This "backward" section was placed in the Charter as a "way out" clause in order to gain the support of the provincial governments for the new Constitution. Under this section the provinces do not have to adhere to particular sections of the Charter if they do not agree with their practical application. However, a government that invokes section 33 concerning a particular piece of legislation is likely to feel the wrath of the voters on the next election day.

The government of Quebec, which was the only province not to sign the Constitution Act, 1982, invoked the notwithstanding clause in regard to its French-language law, Bill 101. This law limits the language of business advertising in Quebec and is a violation of freedom of expression (fundamental freedoms); thus, it is only enforceable if section 33 is invoked. Section 1 of the Charter could not save Bill 101 as a reasonable limit. Some Quebecers believe that Canada's justice minister should create a new anti-gang law to criminalize association with an illegal motorcycle gang. Such a law would obviously violate the Charter's freedom of association section and would only be enforceable if section 33 of the Charter were invoked, since it would not likely be considered a reasonable limit under section 1. It appears the federal government is not contemplating such a drastic move. The notwithstanding clause has been used in a few circumstances, and its use is not likely to increase.

What happens when the Charter is violated and sections 1 and 33 have not been invoked?

Violating someone's Charter rights is not considered in and of itself an offence, criminal or otherwise. However, if the right was violated to a severe degree, then possibly the person who violated the right has committed an offence. For example, if subsequent to an arrest a security officer uses excessive force when conducting a search, then section 8 of the Charter has probably been violated. As a result of this excessive force, the security officer may well face criminal charges as well as civil liability. Violating a Charter right is not necessarily an offence; but a criminal offence and/or civil liability may possibly arise out of the circumstances in which the Charter was violated. However, if a security guard violated only the right to counsel (s.10(b)), it is difficult to imagine what criminal offence could arise from the situation.

The penalties, if you will, that are found in the Charter are located in section 24. This section reads as follows:

24. (1) Anyone whose rights or freedoms, as guaranteed by this Charter, have been infringed or denied may apply to a court of competent jurisdiction to obtain such remedy as the court considers appropriate and just in the circumstances.

(2) Where, in proceedings under subsection (1), a court concludes that evidence was obtained in a manner that infringed or denied any rights or freedoms guaranteed by this Charter, the evidence shall be excluded if it is established that, having regard to all the circumstances, the admission of it in the proceedings would bring the administration of justice into disrepute.

Very simply put, section 24(1) allows the court, if a Charter right has been violated, to render a remedy such as the extreme step of granting a dismissal or stay of proceedings. A stay of proceedings, which is favourable to the accused, is short of a dismissal since the Crown may within a certain time frame proceed to trial again. Also, under section 24(2) the court may exclude evidence that was obtained as a result of the Charter violation. This happens more often than the imposition of a stay of proceedings. Whether evidence is excluded depends on whether the court's reputation will be tainted. For the court's reputation to be tainted, the Charter violation must have occurred either before or during evidence collection. For example, if an accused was purposely denied his or her right to counsel upon arrest so that the investigator could obtain an incriminating statement, the admission of the statement would probably bring the administration of justice into disrepute. Of course, this is only a general hypothesis; each case is decided on its own circumstances. Often, evidence is *not* excluded under 24(2) even if the Charter has been violated before or during evidence collection, when admitting the evidence would not bring the administration of justice into disrepute. When the evidence is physical or real (such as a knife or a gun), it is more likely to be admitted in spite of a Charter violation than if it was self-incriminating (such as a confession). The reasoning here is that the physical evidence would likely have been found regardless of the violation, whereas the self-incriminating evidence would not have been. See *R. v. Collins* (1987) 33 C.C.C. (3d) 1 (S.C.C.) for the Supreme Court of Canada guidelines in making decisions under section 24(2).

CRIMINAL LAW

Most security personnel require a thorough knowledge of their legal authority under the Criminal Code. The definition of a criminal offence used in this book is as follows: "a violation of a federal statute that is designated as a crime."

A criminal offence can only be found in a federal statute because our Constitution gave the federal government the sole authority to create such offences. The second aspect of the above definition points to the fact that for a crime to have been committed, violating the federal statute must be designated as a crime. There are many federal statutes the violation of which does not result in a criminal offence—for example, federal regulatory offences. Refer to the following list for some of the federal statutes the violation of which is considered a crime.

- Criminal Code (CC)
- Narcotic Control Act (NCA—to be replaced by Controlled Drugs and Substances Act)
- Young Offenders Act (YOA)
- Immigration Act of Canada
- Customs Act
- Income Tax Act
- Food and Drugs Act (FDA)
- Firearms Act (FA—not in force yet)

Since most of Canada's criminal offences and procedures are found in the Criminal Code, I will focus on this statute when explaining criminal law in reference to security personnel.

All criminal offences belong to one of three categories:

- Summary
- Indictable
- Dual

The Criminal Code indicates which of the three categories deals with a certain offence. From a security perspective, the main reason to be aware of the offence classifications is to more readily determine when an arrest can be made. **Summary** offences are considered less serious crimes; for these the maximum penalty, with a few exceptions, is a $2000 fine and/or 6 months in jail. **Indictable** offences are more serious; for these the maximum penalty is listed under each specific offence in the Code. Since Canada does not have capital punishment, the maximum penalty for an indictable offence such as murder is life imprisonment. **Dual** (or hybrid) offences, as the name suggests, permit the Crown to choose whether to proceed against the accused summarily or on indictment. In the Criminal Code you will not see the word "dual" (or hybrid); rather you will find, listed below the offence, the penalty as being an indictable offence (with the maximum penalty mentioned) *or* punishable on summary conviction. These offences are always treated as indictable until the Crown decides otherwise. This is an important point to remember concerning powers of arrest for both police and private security officers. The exception to the above maximum summary penalty applies to certain dual offences where the Crown decides to proceed by way of summary conviction. The maximum summary penalty in these specific offences has recently been increased to 18 months from 6 months. Some of the dual offences that include this increased summary penalty component are uttering threats to cause death or bodily harm, sexual assault, and assault with a weapon or causing bodily harm.

Other differences between summary and indictable offences relate to the statute of limitations and to court procedures. In regard to the statute of limitations, before a trial can commence an information must be laid. This **information** consists basically of an informant (usually a police officer, but it could be anyone, including security personnel) going before a justice of the peace and stating, under oath and in writing, that there are reasonable grounds to believe that someone has committed a criminal offence. This information must be laid before any criminal trial can commence. For summary offences this information must be laid within six months from the time the offence occurred. For indictable offences there is no such time limit. Dual offences are assumed to be indictable until the Crown decides otherwise; this means that even if the Crown ultimately proceeds by way of summary conviction on a dual offence, there is still no time limit for laying the information.

The term **reasonable grounds** (once referred to as reasonable and probable grounds) can be described as some evidence that would lead a rational, logical, and moral person to believe something beyond mere suspicion (or with a degree of certainty), such as beyond rumour, gossip, or a hunch (Arcaro, 1994: 8, *Hicks v. Faulkner*, 1882). In other words, reasonable grounds are more than just a "gut feeling"; they must be based on a degree of evidence. For example, just seeing a person with a known criminal record across the street from a residence where a recent break-and-enter occurred would not, by itself, constitute reasonable grounds. On the other hand, reasonable grounds could be developed if the suspect could be identified by a credible witness or by other evidence such as finding stolen property from the house in the suspect's possession. Other evidence that may establish reasonable grounds is any self-incriminating statement made by the suspect, since no law prohibits anyone from having a voluntary conversation with the suspect even if there are no reasonable grounds. The courts have the ultimate authority to determine whether reasonable grounds exist. The term "reasonable" is an important concept that you will encounter everywhere in the criminal and private law.

Court procedures vary with the offence. For most indictable offences the accused may elect the mode of trial. In Ontario the following three options are open to such an accused:

1. General Division Court Judge and Jury.

2. General Division Court Judge.

3. Provincial Court Judge.

Options 1 and 2 allow the accused a preliminary hearing. The purpose of this hearing is to determine whether there is sufficient evidence to warrant a trial. The Crown and the defence may call witnesses during this hearing. For accused persons, two advantages of a preliminary hearing are that they can hear some of the evidence against them, and that the whole case may be dismissed if the Crown fails to show that there is sufficient evidence to proceed to trial. Option 1 permits the accused to have a jury decide the facts of the case. Whether an accused selects this option usually depends on the crime charged: some crimes will evoke more sympathy from a jury than others. Option 3 does not allow the accused a preliminary hearing. However, this option is usually less backlogged, and so the case is more likely to be heard expeditiously.

For offences under sections 469 and 553 of the Criminal Code, there are exceptions to the election rules. Section 469 deals with very serious offences such as murder and treason, for which the accused must generally be tried by a judge and jury. Section 553 offences are less serious, nonviolent offences, such as theft, fraud, and possession of stolen property under $5 000. An accused charged with an indictable offence under this section does not have an election and must go before a Provincial Court judge. Presumably, when the system removes the accused's right to a preliminary hearing or jury trial, it runs more smoothly and cheaply. With summary offences, the accused has no election and must go before a Provincial Court judge, for the same reasons that applied to section 553 offences.

Table 3.3 classifies some of the offences in the Criminal Code.

ARREST/DETENTION

Definitions

Before we examine the legal authority that allows security personnel to make arrests, you must fully understand when an arrest or detention has taken place. In regard to private citizens making arrests, the law is clear: the Charter of Rights and Freedoms applies. In other words, when an arrest is made the arrested person must be informed of the reason for the arrest (s.10(a)) and of his or her right to counsel (s.10(b)). Both of these elements will be discussed later in this chapter. For the purposes of instruction, it is best to view arrest and detention as two ends of a continuum.

Generally (but not necessarily), an arrest involves removing someone's freedom or liberty by physical control. This action may include verbally telling the person that he or she

TABLE 3.3	Select Criminal Offences	
SUMMARY	**DUAL**	**INDICTABLE**
• Causing disturbance (s.175)	• Assault (s.266)	• Aggravated assault (s.268)
• Cruelty to animals (s.446)	• Assaulting a peace officer (s.270 (1a))	• Aggravated sexual assault (s.273)
• Failure to keep watch on people towed (i.e. water-skiing) (s.250)	• Assaulting person with intent to resist arrest (s.270(1b))	• Break and enter (s.348)
• Found in common bawdy-house (s.210(2))	• Carrying concealed weapon (s.89)	• Bribery of officers (s.120)
• Found in common gaming or betting house (s.201(2))	• Criminal harassment (s.264)	• Fraud over $5000 (s.380)
• Indecent acts (s.173)	• Dangerous operation of vehicle (involving no bodily harm or death) (s.249)	• Hostage taking (s.279.1)
• Indecent/harassing phone calls (s.372 (2), (3))	• Failure to stop at scene of accident (s.252)	• Kidnapping (s.279)
• Intimidation (s.423)	• False alarm of fire (s.437)	• Murder (s.229)
• Joyriding (s.335)	• Fraud under $5000 (s.380)	• Perjury (s.131)
• Nudity (s.174)	• Impaired driving (s.253)	• Possession of counterfeit money (s.450)
• Offensive volatile substance (s.178)	• Mischief under or over $5000 (s.430)	• Possession of weapon or imitation (s.87)
• Personating peace officer (s.130)	• Over 80 (s.253)	• Theft over $5000 (s.322, s.334)
• Personation at examination (s. 404)	• Pointing a firearm (s.86)	
• Prostitution (soliciting) (s.213)	• Possession of unregistered restricted weapon (s.91)	
• Trespass at night (s.177)	• Possession of prohibited weapon (s.90)	
• Unlawful assembly (s.63)	• Public mischief (s.140)	
	• Sexual assault (s.271)	
	• Theft under $5000 (s.322, s.334)	
	• Uttering threats (s.264.1)	

is under arrest, as well as a reasonable amount of force to show physical control (such as lightly grasping the person by the arm). An arrest can also take place without actual physical contact where the person submits or acquiesces upon notification of the arrest. An arrest can even take place where there is no physical contact and the word "arrest" is never mentioned. In *R. v. J.A.* (1992) in the Ontario Unified Family Court, an arrest was deemed to have taken place when a building superintendent, along with security personnel, blocked the exits to prevent a group of four youths from leaving. The superintendent then demanded that they answer his questions about the content of their bags. In other words, a person who is not aware of the laws can arrest someone quite unintentionally. In the above case, stolen property was found in the bags but was excluded as evidence under section 24(2) of the Charter. This exclusion ultimately led to an acquittal of the youths on the charge of possession of stolen property.

A detention can occur without the detainee being placed under physical restraint. The Supreme Court of Canada in *R. v. Therens* (1985) 18 C.C.C. (3d) 481 (S.C.C.) ruled that a detention "refers to a restraint of liberty of varying duration other than arrest" (p. 481). This detention can occur through psychological coercion where "the person concerned submits or acquiesces in the deprivation of liberty and reasonably believes that the choice to do otherwise does not exist" (p. 505). Thus, a detention exists when a person (such as a security guard) controls another person by demand or direction, or when the detainee feels a psychological compulsion, believing that freedom of liberty has been removed. For example, a detention may occur if a person is told to come to a security office for questioning and upon entering, the door is shut by the security officer, though left unlocked. That person may very well feel unable to leave; see *R. v. Shafie* (1989) 47 C.C.C. (3d) 27 (Ont. C.A.). The difficulty with a detention is that it can evolve to an arrest depending on how the circumstances unfold. As already noted, the direct application of physical force is not always needed to bring about an arrest, nor are spoken words such as *you are under arrest* required. In *R. v. MacDonald* (1974) 22 C.C.C. (2d) 350 (N.S.C.A.), Macdonald J.A. reported at p. 356 that "although arrest includes detention, detention does not necessarily include arrest." Security personnel must understand how a detention can escalate into an arrest; there is potential liability if an arrest is made unlawfully, even if unintentionally.

Charter Applicability

Does the charter apply to actions of private security personnel when conducting arrests and detentions?

Arrests The simple answer is, it depends. It appears from recent case law that when private citizens arrest someone they are deemed to be performing a governmental action that subsequently triggers Charter involvement; see *R. v. Lerke* (1986) 24 C.C.C. (3d) 129, Alb. C.A., and *R. v. Dean* (1991) 5 C.R. (4th) 176 (Ont. Ct. of Justice). Concerning *Lerke*, Laycraft CJ.A. said at p. 134 of the judgment that "the arrest of a citizen is a governmental function whether the person making the arrest is a peace officer or a private citizen." The importance to private security of this finding is that the arrested person is entitled to constitutional rights found in the Charter such as the right to counsel without delay. As well, other rights (s.8, protection against unreasonable searches), if violated at the time of arrest, may lead to evidence under section 24(2) being excluded.

Detentions Detentions by private persons seem not to be considered a governmental function and therefore do not automatically trigger the Charter's involvement. In *R. v. Shafie* (1989) 47 C.C.C. (3d) 27 (Ont. C.A.), an employer who was experiencing unexplained losses to his business hired a private investigator to find out who was responsible for those losses. In the course of the investigation the private investigator interviewed employees from the business. One employee, Shafie, was told by the employer to speak to the private investigator. Shafie did so and subsequently gave incriminating evidence. Krever J.A. determined that this was a detention. However, more importantly, he further stated that a detention by private persons does not constitute a detention under section 10 of the Charter because such a detention is not authorized by law and therefore does not trigger its application. He further stated at p. 32 that the Charter "does apply in the case of a citizen's arrest because the action of arresting, even by a private citizen, if it is authorized by law, is taken on behalf of the state." In other words, since a detention by a citizen is not authorized by a particular statute, it is not a governmental action. However, a peace officer detaining someone is always considered to be performing a governmental action, and the Charter would apply. Overall, the issue is this: If a detention did in fact occur, was it a detention covered under section 10 of the Charter?

One might argue that a detention initiated by a security officer is not governmental action at first, but because evidence is found (such as statements) that may be used in a subsequent prosecution by the state, it ultimately becomes a governmental action. Krever responded to this argument by stating at p. 34 that "the question whether a person's s. 10(b) rights were infringed must be tested as at the time the alleged detention occurred." Also, "any other conclusion would result in the judicialization of private relationships beyond the point that society could tolerate. The requirement that advice about the right to counsel must be given by a school teacher to a pupil, by an employer to an employee or a parent to a child, to mention only a few relationships, is difficult to contemplate" (p. 34). However, a detention by private security personnel could conceivably be considered a governmental action if the security person was acting under the direction of a police officer. This situation could develop if police sought to circumvent the Charter by asking private security/citizens to detain and elicit responses from a suspect.

ARREST AUTHORITY

Two primary statutes that allow private citizens, including private security, to make arrests are the Criminal Code and the various trespass to property acts. The latter vary between provinces, and this may affect arrest authority. Some of the provincial highway traffic acts also allow citizens to make arrests for certain offences. This type of legislation, however, is used to a much lesser extent by private security than the first two types.

All security personnel who may make arrests should thoroughly understand section 494 of the Criminal Code.

s. 494 (private citizen's power of arrest)

(1) Any one may arrest without warrant

   (a) a person whom he finds committing an indictable offence; or

   (b) a person who, on reasonable grounds, he believes

      (i) has committed a criminal offence, and

      (ii) is escaping from and freshly pursued by persons who have lawful authority to arrest that person.

(2) Any one who is

   (a) the owner or a person in lawful possession of property, or

   (b) a person authorized by the owner or by a person in lawful possession of property may arrest without warrant a person whom he finds committing a criminal offence on or in relation to property.

(3) Any one other than a peace officer who arrests a person without warrant shall forthwith deliver the person to a peace officer.

A full explanation of section 494 follows.

(1) Any one may arrest without warrant

    (a) a person whom he finds committing an indictable offence; or

You now know what an arrest is, and what an indictable offence is. Now you must learn the term "finds committing." **Finds committing** means that you have seen the offence take place with your own eyes and have basically not lost sight of the accused since then. Arcaro (1994: 11) defines "finds committing" as "(a) witnessing the crime actually occur and immediately apprehending the offender, and (b) witnessing the crime actually occur and apprehending the offender after pursuing him or her without losing sight of the offender at any time." Say, for example, you observed a woman in a retail store concealing a Walkman in her coat pocket and exiting without paying. Assume further that while you attempted to arrest her outside in the parking lot, the accused was out of your sight for several minutes, having ducked down an alley. Here, "finds committing" does not apply, and you cannot arrest the woman. Courts have not identified precisely how long it is acceptable for you to lose sight of the accused; their judgments rely instead on the facts and circumstances of individual cases. The alternative in this particular situation is to write down a description and then transfer reasonable grounds to a police officer, who can then make the arrest. Police arrest authority will be discussed later in this chapter.

    (b) a person, who, on reasonable grounds, he believes

        (i) has committed a criminal offence, and

        (ii) is escaping from and freshly pursued by persons who have lawful authority to arrest that person

Reasonable grounds, which was explained earlier, means that there is some evidence which would lead a logical, rational, and prudent person to believe beyond mere suspicion (or beyond a "gut" feeling/rumour) the points outlined in b(i) and b(ii). The phrase "has committed a criminal offence" means that the offence has already occurred; thus, "finds committing" would not apply. "Criminal offence" refers to both summary and indictable offences (including, obviously, dual offences), not just indictable offences as stated in s.494(1)(a). The next important word is "and" because if security made an arrest on reasonable grounds alone—perhaps by reading s.494(1)(b)(i) without including s.494(1)(b)(ii)—it would be considered unlawful. The second aspect of this subsection means that whoever is trying to arrest the person (the primary arrestor) must have lawful authority to make an arrest and be "freshly" pursuing the person in question. This section is really a "help your fellow neighbour" law. Even if the primary arrestor did not have lawful authority to arrest, as long as the person aiding the primary arrestor can fulfil the above requirements based on reasonable grounds, that person will most likely be protected from liability. However, the primary arrestor may not be protected if not acting with lawful authority when arresting. Clearly, conducting an arrest under this section necessarily requires at least three people: the accused, the primary arrestor, and the person aiding primary arrestor.

(2) Any one who is

    (a) the owner or a person in lawful possession of property, or

    (b) a person authorized by the owner or by a person in lawful possession of property may arrest without warrant a person whom he finds committing a criminal offence on or in relation to that property.

This section provides broader powers for security personnel to make arrests. "Owner or a person in lawful possession of property" is self-explanatory. The next "person" is one who is authorized by either the owner or the lawful possessor. Typically, this category would include security personnel; for example, floorwalkers in a retail store would be authorized by the owner. The next aspect of this section is similar to s.494(1)(a) but refers to "finds committing" a criminal offence versus solely an indictable offence; the offence has to occur on or in relation to the property under authorized protection. Again, "criminal offence" can be either summary or indictable or dual.

All private citizens or non-peace officers must turn the arrested person over to the police as soon as practicable, as noted in the following section:

> (3) Any one other than a peace officer who arrests a person without warrant shall forthwith deliver the person to a peace officer.

This section has been interpreted to mean that police should be called to the location of arrest to assume control of the person arrested, instead of the citizen making the arrest physically transporting the arrestee to the police station. Note that according to this section, once a citizen's arrest has been made the arrestor (here, the security) has no legal authority to release the arrested person other than to a peace officer. In other words, if a security officer makes a mistake and arrests someone who was not actually found committing an offence, this officer does not technically have the authority to release the wrongly arrested person back into the community. The only option is still to call the police, who will in turn release the arrested person unconditionally. There is no question that the security officer could be held civilly liable for false imprisonment, but by releasing the person before police arrive he or she could be inviting further liability. The important point here is to make sure that you are arresting under lawful authority. If you are in doubt about the circumstances—for example, if you did not observe the offence actually being committed—the best practice, obviously, is not to make an arrest.

s.495 (peace officer's power of arrest)

For comparative purposes, the main arresting authority for *peace officers* comes from section 495 of the Criminal Code.

> (1) A peace officer may arrest without warrant
>
>   (a) a person who has committed an indictable offence or who, on reasonable grounds, he believes has committed or is about to commit an indictable offence,
>
>   (b) a person whom he finds committing a criminal offence, or
>
>   (c) a person in respect of whom he has reasonable grounds to believe that a warrant of arrest ...

Section 495(2) further limits the above authority to arrest by stating that peace officers shall not arrest without warrant for section 553 indictable offences, dual offences, or summary offences if all of the following (referred to as the abbreviation R.I.C.E.) can be established on reasonable grounds in the interest of the public:

- Prevent **R**epetition of offence.
- **I**dentity of the person.
- Will come to **C**ourt.
- **E**vidence.

In other words, since the above offences are not considered the most serious, the onus is on the peace officer to release the accused, having arranged an appearance notice, or having ensured that a summons is issued. However, be aware that during this process of establishing R.I.C.E. and issuing an appearance notice, the accused has likely been placed under arrest and must be treated accordingly (cautioned, given the right to counsel, and so on).

The basic difference between private security powers of arrest and those of peace officers is that peace officers can arrest on reasonable grounds for indictable offences that were committed in the past or will be committed in the future. Peace officers do not always need to "find commit" in order to arrest for indictable offences; everyone else does. (For a limited exception to this, see section 494.1(b) of the Criminal Code.) Another difference is that peace officers may make an arrest anywhere they "find commit" a summary offence; whereas citizens or security officers can only arrest in regard to property that they either own or are authorized to protect. Remember that since section 494 refers to anyone, this also includes peace officers. Tables 3.4 and 3.5 illustrate the differences in powers of arrest between peace officers and citizens.

TABLE 3.4   Citizens' Powers of Arrest (s.494)

TIME OFFENCE OCCURRED	TYPE OF OFFENCE	
	SUMMARY	INDICTABLE*
Past	No (unless s.494(1)(b)—R/G criminal offence and being pursued by someone with lawful authority to arrest)	No (unless s.494(1)(b))
Present (find commit)	No (unless s.494(2)(a)(b)—if owner or authorized (security) in relation to property)	Yes
Future	No	No

*Remember all dual offences are considered indictable until the Crown decides otherwise

TABLE 3.5   Peace Officers' Powers of Arrest (s.495)

TIME OFFENCE OCCURRED	TYPE OF OFFENCE	
	SUMMARY	INDICTABLE*
Past	No (unless s.494(1)(b))	Yes
Present	Yes (if R.I.C.E. not established)	Yes (if not a s.553 or dual offence or if so, where R.I.C.E. not established)
Future	No	Yes (if not a s.553 or dual offence or if so, where R.I.C.E. not established)

*Remember all dual offences are considered indictable until the Crown decides otherwise

REGULATORY OFFENCES

Aside from the Criminal Code, there are provincial laws that may allow private citizens (which includes security personnel) to make arrests. In Ontario the Trespass to Property Act (TPA) and Highway Traffic Act (HTA) allow for such action. The TPA is by far the most prominent provincial statute that private security personnel—especially those dealing with the public—make use of in carrying out their functions. Most trespassing statutes are quite similar to each other; even so, check the specific authority in your province.

Trespass to Property Act (R.S.O., 1990)

The reader must understand the terms "occupier" and "premises." An **occupier** is defined in section 1 of the act as a person in physical possession of premises (that is, an owner), or a person who has responsibility for and control over the condition of premises *or* the activities carried on there *or* control over persons allowed to enter the premises (including security). In other words, an occupier could be any one of the following categories:

- Owner
- A person who manages property
- Tenants in a building
- Employees
- **Security personnel**

Premises

Premises is defined in section 2 as follows:

lands or structures, or either of them, and includes

- water
- ships and vessels
- trailers and portable structures designed or used for residence, business or shelter
- trains, railway cars, vehicles and aircraft, except while in operation

Premises, therefore, consists of buildings, including businesses or residences, as well as real property such as land.

Offences

The offences under the TPA are found in section 2.

s. 2 (1) Every person who is not acting under a right or authority conferred by law and who,

(a) without the express permission of the occupier, the proof of which rests on the defendant,

(i) enters on premises when entry is prohibited under this Act, or

(ii) engages in an activity on premises when the activity is prohibited under this Act; or

(b) does not leave the premises immediately after he or she is directed to do so by the occupier of the premises or a person authorized by the occupier,

is guilty of an offence and on conviction is liable to a fine of not more than $2000.

The first question that comes to mind is how one is to give notice that an entry or activity is prohibited. Section 5 of the act describes four methods:

Orally —that is, verbally telling someone to leave the property immediately or that the particular conduct is prohibited.

In writing —that is, sending a person a registered letter stating that he or she is no longer allowed on the property.

By signs —placing at a point of access a sign on which the forbidden activity is named or graphically displayed, with an oblique line through it.

By marking systems—having at a point of access a red dot at least 10 centimetres in diameter.

If the premises is a public place, such as a retail store or casino, the public is generally allowed access unless otherwise stated. If a person is told to leave (or informed in writing not to return) and does not leave immediately (or returns), this person is deemed to have violated the TPA. Unfortunately, the TPA does not provide sufficiently clear guidelines as to when someone can be asked to leave. Other types of legislation, such as provincial human rights laws, fill this void to the extent that they affect decisions made under the TPA. For example, consider a retail store policy stating that anybody entering the premises with a weapon (or something that could reasonably be used as such) will be asked to leave unless the weapon is left behind. A violation of the Ontario Human Rights Code would occur if practising Sikhs entered the premises with ceremonial daggers (or kirpans) and were told to leave the daggers at the door or otherwise be denied entry. This suggests why security personnel should keep informed of changes in human rights laws. A related example is the recent 1997 court ruling in British Columbia that protects a mother's right to breast-feed her infant in public. Blind reliance on policy will not be a valid defence for security personnel if their actions contravene legislation such as human rights codes.

In some circumstances entry can be prohibited without any notice—for example, if someone is found in the occupier's garden, field, or other land under cultivation (which can be a lawn, an orchard, or a vineyard). Also, enclosed premises, including fenced ones, indicate the occupier's intention to keep people off or animals within. Note well that section 3(2) of the act states that "there is a presumption that access for lawful purposes to the door of a building on premises by a means apparently provided and used for the purpose of access is not prohibited." In other words, if someone uses your driveway and walkway to approach your house, there is no violation of this act because there is an implication that this area can be used legally (including for soliciting) unless otherwise stated. However, once the person has been told to leave, the person in question must leave immediately or risk violating the TPA. Whoever walks on your lawn (or land under cultivation), without permission, has *technically* violated the act even if there has been no formal warning. In this type of common and nonthreatening situation, one is obviously not encouraged to make an arrest.

Citizens' Authority When TPA Violated?

A citizen's authority to arrest comes from section 9 of the act as follows:

9(1) A police officer, or the occupier of premises, or a person authorized by the occupier may arrest without warrant any person he or she believes on reasonable and probable grounds to be on the premises in contravention of section 2.

(2) Where the person who makes an arrest under subsection (1) is not a police officer, he or she shall promptly call for assistance of a police officer and give the person arrested into the custody of the police officer.

Under section 9(1) the occupier or someone authorized by the occupier (including a security guard) is entitled to arrest. Here, consider the phrase "reasonable and probable grounds" as meaning the same as "find committing," discussed earlier. Like section 494 of the Criminal Code, section 9(2) states that all non–police officers who make an arrest under the TPA shall turn the arrested person over to police.

Highway Traffic Act (R.S.O., 1990)

We will look at Ontario's Highway Traffic Act (HTA) in regard to its impact on private security's ability to make arrests. The highway acts vary from province to province, so security personnel should make themselves familiar with the laws in their jurisdictions. Note that while the HTA gives private citizens (including security) the authority to make arrests, such arrests are seldom made. Arrests are more likely to be made under the Criminal Code or the Trespass to Property Act. However, many traditional functions of government are now being privatized, and in this climate private toll highways are being developed (Ontario's new Highway 407 being the best known). In the future, these types of highways may very well need the private sector to complement government enforcement units, and this will require a thorough understanding of provincial HTAs.

The term "highway" refers to areas intended for use by the general public for the passage of vehicles; it does not include private property. Section 217 of the HTA lists the offences that police officers may use to arrest on reasonable grounds and that private citizens (including security personnel) may use to arrest when they "find commit." Table 3.6 contains a list of the offences that private citizens may employ to make an arrest when they find a person committing the offence. For the exact wording of each of these offences, refer to the HTA.

SEARCH AUTHORITY

Searching authority for private citizens, and in turn private security, is found mainly within the common law. In other words, authority for private citizens to search is not found in the statutes, with a few limited exceptions. I have divided this authority to search into two categories: *with consent* and *without consent*. After an arrest, an accused can be searched either by consent or if there is reason to believe that a weapon is involved. The accused should not be searched without consent for evidence only. Without an arrest, a person can be searched by consent, or their property can be searched to a degree through an implied consent, such as an employee contract.

Searching Without Consent

When does the Charter right to freedom from unreasonable search (s.8) apply to private citizen or security officer searches? The answer seems to correspond with the previous explanations concerning the relationship between arrests and the Charter. Since arrests by private citizens are considered a governmental function, it would logically follow that searches incidental to the arrest would be considered a governmental function, thus triggering the application of the Charter. At the same time, if security officers searched someone who had not been arrested, then this action would be a non-Charter issue. In other words, the Charter does not apply if security officers are performing a nongovernmental function—such as searching an employee—without an arrest, under the authority of the employee's contract (see the section on consent searches).

TABLE 3.6	Offences under Ontario's HTA Allowing Citizen's Arrest
SECTION	**DESCRIPTION**
9(1)	• Making false statement on application, declaration, affidavit, or paper writing required under the HTA.
12(1)	• Violations to plates/validation, including defacing, altering, removing plate without authority, or using plate/validation without authority.
13(1)	• Confuse identity of number plate.
33(3)	• Refusal by driver to provide licence to police officer when requested.
47(5), (6), (7), (8)	• Unlawful possession or applying for owner's permit when suspended.
	• Apply for/possession of driver's licence when suspended.
	• Applies for commercial vehicle licence when suspended.
	• Drives commercial vehicle while suspended.
51	• Drives motor vehicle while permit is suspended.
53	• Drives motor vehicle on highway while licence is suspended.
130	• Driving carelessly on highway.
172	• Racing on highway.
184	• Defacing or removing notices or obstructions on highway.
185(3)	• Refuse to accompany police officer off highway that is prohibited to pedestrians.
200(1a)	• Fail to remain at scene of accident that occurred on highway.
216(1)	• Driver fails to stop when requested by police officer.

In *R. v. Lerke* (1986) 43 Alta. L.R. (2d), 1 (Alta. C.A.), an accused was searched without consent after being arrested under the provincial trespassing laws. Lerke, the accused, had been asked to leave a tavern earlier because the tavern manager thought he was under age and because he did not produce identification to indicate otherwise. The accused re-entered the tavern later that night and was arrested and then searched for evidence of identification. During this nonconsensual search, narcotics were found in the accused's jacket. After the police responded, he was charged with possession of narcotics (and also a liquor offence). The arrest in this situation, which was considered a governmental action, was considered valid under Alberta's trespassing law. However, the nonconsensual search for identification that uncovered narcotics was considered unreasonable under section 8 of the Charter, for the following reasons:

• There was no nexus between the search for proof of age and the trespassing offence, since trespassing had been committed regardless of age once Lerke re-entered after being asked to leave.

• There was no state of urgency that required searching the accused before the police arrived (neither the tavern owner nor the police believed that Lerke was considered dangerous).

Because of the section 8 violation, the narcotics evidence was excluded under section 24(2), since it would have brought the administration of justice into disrepute. It seems from this case that searching for evidence (as opposed to weapons) by private citizens is not automatic (as it is for the police) and therefore must meet a higher threshold of reasonableness under section 8. The judgment in this case was delivered by Laycraft C.J.A., who stated (p. 13):

> Where the search is not for weapons, but only to seize or preserve property connected to the offence, different considerations apply. The urgency present in the search for weapons would not ordinarily be present in those cases. Often the triviality of the offence charged or the improbability, in the circumstances, that any evidence will be uncovered, or will be destroyed even if search is delayed, will mean that the search by a citizen would not be a reasonable search.

Justice Laycraft further stated (p. 13) that "it will be rare that the citizen making an arrest will need to search for evidentiary purposes only." Thus, searches for evidence should usually be left for police officers. Police, on the other hand, can search automatically under common law as long as the search is deemed reasonable under section 8 of the Charter; see *Langlois and Bedard v. Cloutier* (1990) 74 C.R. (3d) 316 (S.C.C.). An example of an unreasonable search after an arrest is when the police conduct a search in order to intimidate the accused and are not searching for weapons or evidence. In other words, the search by police officers incidental to an arrest, if done in "good faith," seems to be an automatic right, unlike that of private citizens.

Private security personnel should only conduct a nonconsensual search incidental to arrest if weapons are believed to be present (see below), or presumably if the circumstances are such that evidence might be destroyed by the accused before police arrive.

Armed with Weapon

It seems that under common law, if security personnel have reason to believe that the arrested person is armed with a weapon that could possibly cause harm, they have the right to search for that weapon. Unfortunately, there seems to be no legal definition of "reason to believe." Presumably, security personnel would be safer from a legal standpoint if "reason to believe" was equated with "reasonable grounds." In the end, the decision to search for a weapon is at the sole discretion of the individual security officer who is in possible harm's way. Each situation needs to be judged on its own merits. What led the security guard to believe that the arrested person might be armed with a weapon? Was it a visual sighting, or statements made by the accused or witnesses, or the accused's history? Presumably, the courts will protect security personnel who conduct weapons searches in good faith.

The next logical question is this: What happens if you stumble across evidence of a crime while searching for a weapon? Despite the lack of any case law to definitively answer this question, I would presume that the person conducting the search could then seize the evidence, as it would have been found during a lawful search. It is important to point out that it would need to be apparent to a reasonable person that the arrested subject might be armed with a weapon. Otherwise, a security officer could simply search anyone arrested under the guise that there might be a weapon involved. The apparent rationale behind limiting a citizen's authority to search an accused after an arrest is that if there is no perceived danger, then there is no urgency to search. The accused should remain under the citizen's control until the arrival of police, who have the automatic authority to search.

With a Warrant

The Criminal Code has recently been changed to allow "a person" or a peace officer to conduct a search that has been authorized by a warrant. This inclusion of "a person" is highly unusual, in that someone other than a peace officer (such as private security) could apply for this warrant. The procedures involving these warrants are found in sections 492.1(1) and 492.2(1). The former deals mainly with the installation, maintenance, monitoring, and removal of "tracking devices." Tracking devices are defined as "any device that, when installed in or on any thing, may be used to help ascertain, by electronic or other means, the location of any thing or person"; see section 492.1(4). Section 492.2(1) deals with the installation, maintenance, monitoring, and removal of number recorders. Number recorders are defined as "any device that can be used to record or identify the telephone number or location of the telephone from which a telephone call originates, or at which it is received or is intended to be received"; see section 492.2(4). Section 492.2(2) also permits a judge to order "any person or body that lawfully possesses records of telephone calls" (for example, telephone companies) to give the records to the person named in the order.

Conceivably, private security personnel can apply for both the tracking device and number recorder warrants if they have reasonable grounds to suspect that a criminal offence has been or will be committed and that further relevant information will be provided by these means. I have not seen any case law on these new procedures but would expect an increase in their use by private citizens.

Searching With Consent

Consent searches are a valuable tool for both police and private security personnel. Since a private citizen's arrest is considered a governmental function that triggers the application of the Charter, any violation of someone's section 8 rights during a search may result in evidence being excluded under section 24(2). However, when private citizens are engaged in searches when they are not considered state agents (that is, when they are not performing governmental functions such as arrests, and when they are not working under the direction of police officers), the repercussions of improper searches become less clear. Even when section 8 and ultimately section 24(2) do not apply in this scenario, other laws, both criminal and civil, may apply.

Consent searches by private citizens have not been thoroughly defined in case law. However, in *R. v. Wills* (1992) 70 C.C.C. (3d) 529 (Ont. C.A.), Justice Doherty J.A. wrote (p. 546) that the Crown must establish, on a balance of probabilities, that the police search was truly consensual. For this to be so, the following must be true:

    (i)   there was consent, express or implied;

    (ii) the giver of consent had the authority to give the consent in question;

    (iii) the consent was voluntary in the sense that [the] word ... was not the product of police oppression, coercion or other external conduct which negated the freedom to choose whether or not to allow the police to pursue the course of conduct requested;

    (iv) the giver of consent was aware of the nature of the police conduct to which he or she was being asked to consent;

    (v) the giver of consent was aware of his or her right to refuse to permit the police to engage in the conduct requested, and

    (vi) the giver of the consent was aware of the potential consequences of giving the consent.

By following these guidelines, police would be making it much more likely that their searches were both informed and voluntary. Justice Doherty intended these guidelines to apply to police searches; but it would be prudent for private security to adhere to them as well, especially when criminal charges might eventually result.

Searches are often a condition of entry to premises, such as music concerts, bars, and sporting events. A person who refuses consent to be searched should not be searched, but that person will likely be refused entry, despite having paid already for an entrance ticket.

Employee contracts may allow private security to search employee property, such as handbags and lockers. The consent given by an employee would likely be an implied form of consent since it would be a condition of employment. However, there are limits to this arrangement. A forced search against an employee who revokes consent would be unlawful, even if it was on company property and even if the employee had previously agreed to searches as a condition of employment. The option in this case would be to document the circumstances for superiors, who could then decide what disciplinary action to take (up to dismissal). A forced search against employees, especially if it is a requirement before leaving the property, may very well be considered a criminal assault; at the least it will involve civil liabilities. Another option is to transfer reasonable grounds to police, who can then apply for a search warrant. David Ray (1993: 59) indicates the following guidelines for searching at the work site:

- The search must be reasonable—there must be some evidence that the offence took place and that the search will provide evidence.

- The search policy should be applied consistently and should not target an individual or department.

RIGHT TO COUNSEL AND CAUTION

Right to Counsel

Based on the above case law, the Charter is applicable during citizen's arrests since such arrests are considered a governmental function. Specifically, accused people must be informed of their section 10(a) and (b) rights under the Charter when being arrested by a citizen. The same applies to people being detained or arrested by police officers. Detentions by private citizens are not usually considered a governmental function (unless those detentions are being directed by police officers). Conversely, since police officers are presumed to be agents of the state, any detentions they make will be considered a governmental function and trigger application of the Charter. Sections 10(a) and 10(b) of the Charter read as follows:

10. Everyone has the right on arrest or detention
    (a) to be informed promptly of the reasons therefor;
    (b) to retain and instruct counsel without delay and to be informed of that right

Considering its length (or lack of it), this section—especially section 10(b)—has inspired a significant amount of case law since 1982. A sample of the Right to Counsel used by most Ontario police services is provided later in the chapter. Two further points: First, the Supreme Court of Canada does not list word for word what should be contained in this section, but rather provides guidelines containing elements that must be conveyed. Second, one must stay abreast of recent court decisions concerning this section, which will continue to evolve.

Following are some guidelines that have evolved from case law. Most of this information was gleaned from case law research conducted by Gino Arcaro for Niagara College.

1. *Without delay*

- Means as soon as reasonably possible.

2. *Clearly communicate this right*

- Use exact words from the Charter.

3. *Ensure rights are understood*

- Ask if accused understands. Additional explanation may be necessary.
- Give in language accused understands.
- Must inform accused of 1-800 number (where it exists) regarding the existence of free and immediate legal advice.
- Must inform accused that he/she may be eligible for legal aid (regardless of financial status).

4. *If accused invokes right to counsel*

- Provide opportunity without delay.
- Cease questioning of accused until that opportunity has been provided.
- Allow accused more than one phone call (however, accused must be reasonably diligent in obtaining counsel).
- What happens if accused calls lawyer and waits for answer (that is, leaves a message on lawyer's answering machine)?
  —If accused initiates conversation, then no violation.
  —If police (and presumably private security) initiate conversation, then violation has occurred.
- After accused speaks to lawyer, can police (and presumably private security) question accused?
  —Yes, as long as it was voluntarily inculpable (incriminating) and accused believed he could remain silent
- Right to counsel automatically means the right to privacy. Police or security must accord the right to privacy to the accused; thus, they cannot listen to the accused's conversation with counsel.

5. *If accused chooses not to invoke, or waives right to counsel*

- Waiver must be clear and unequivocal.
- Accused must have full knowledge of the nature and consequences of giving up right (especially if alcohol and drugs are involved).
- Adults can waive their right to counsel verbally (as in "No, I do not want to speak to a lawyer.")
- Young offenders must have a written waiver or be videotaped. Also, they may have an adult or parent/guardian present instead of or with their lawyer, as per Y.O.A.; see sections 11 and 56.

Statements and the Caution

Statements, whether written or oral, can be either inculpatory or exculpatory. **Inculpatory statements** are self-incriminating statements indicative of a person's guilt, and include confessions and admissions. Confessions are statements where an accused admits to committing the entire offence, thus proving all the facts at issue (that is, all the elements of the offence). Admissions fall short of confessions; they are statements where the accused admits to certain facts which may implicate them in a crime. **Exculpatory statements** are statements indicative of a person's innocence, for example, "I was not even in town during this crime, let alone even know the victim."

These statements can be given to either a person in authority or a person not in authority. A **person in authority** is a person whom the accused believes could influence prosecution, whether or not this belief has foundation. Such persons include police officers and Crown attorneys, and sometimes private security personnel making arrests or gathering information that could be forwarded to police. Logically, then, **people not in authority** are people whom the accused believes cannot influence their prosecution. Such people include friends and physicians—also, police informers when the accused does not know that they are affiliated with the police and could influence the prosecution. The courts have made it clear to police that when collecting statements, they cannot act in ways that might shock the community. Thus, a police officer cannot pose as a priest or a psychiatrist to obtain incriminating statements.

The courts have determined that a relevant statement to a person in authority, in order to be admissible, must have been given voluntarily. The idea of voluntariness of statements is rooted in the common law, and is set out in guidelines under the English Judges' Rules (1912) and in *R. v. Ibrahim* (1914), the case from which was derived the Ibrahim Rule. Both of these English rules are often referred to by Canadian courts. As well, sections 7 and 10 of the Charter also incorporate the notion of voluntariness and the right to remain silent.

Voluntariness of statements given to persons in authority is determined through *voir dires*, which are hearings conducted during a trial to determine the admissibility of statements. If the *voir dire* is conducted during a jury trial, the jury will be absent during this hearing, as the admissibility of a statement is determined solely by the judge upon hearing the evidence. If the judge admits the statement, the jury will hear it and then determine its credibility. The onus is on the Crown to prove beyond a reasonable doubt that the statement was voluntary. To determine voluntariness during *voir dire*, the courts "will consider the stage of investigation at which the statement was made, weighing carefully the circumstances or pressures on the person which caused him to speak" (Marin, 1992: 235). "Voluntary" has also been defined as "free from inducement," meaning free from "words or acts that cause an accused person to believe that his or her status will improve or worsen, relating to the charge, depending on whether or not s/he makes a statement" (O.P.C., 1984, as in Arcaro, 1993: 169). In other words, inducements may occur unintentionally. For example, in *R. v. Letendre* (1979), 46 C.C.C. (2d) 398 (B.C.C.A.), a police officer saying to the accused, without raising his voice, the words "Well, I'm getting mad" after he had become frustrated with the accused's answers, constituted an inducement that rendered the accused's inculpatory statement inadmissible.

To reduce inducements, it is recommended that the accused be given a caution (see Figure 3.1). This caution is only a guideline, not a statutory requirement. In *Boudreau v. The King* (1949), 94 C.C.C. 1, the courts said the following (p. 9): "It would be a serious error to place the ordinary modes of investigation of crime in a straight-jacket of artificial rules: and the true protection against improper interrogation or any kind of pressure or inducement is to leave the broad question to the Court."

FIGURE 3.1   Sample Right to Counsel and the Caution

SAMPLE RIGHT TO COUNSEL (ONTARIO)

I am arresting you for _____ [briefly describe reasons].

It is my duty to inform you that you have the right to retain and instruct counsel without delay. You have the right to telephone any lawyer you wish. You also have the right to free advice from a legal aid lawyer. If you are charged with an offence, you may apply to the Ontario Legal Aid Plan for assistance. 1-800-265-0451 is a toll-free number that will put you in contact with a Legal Aid Duty Counsel Lawyer for free legal advice right now.

Do you understand?

Do you wish to call a lawyer right now?

Caution

You may be charged with _____.

Do you wish to say anything in answer to the charge? You are not obliged to say anything unless you wish to do so, but whatever you say may be given in evidence.

Do you understand?

Secondary Caution
(only used when someone else in authority spoke to the accused earlier)

Regardless of anything that anybody has said to you or that you have said to any other person in authority, you are not obliged to say anything unless you wish to do so, but whatever you say may be given in evidence.

Do you understand?

Thus, the caution should be combined with the right to counsel in order to reduce inducements and increase the chances that inculpatory statements will be deemed admissible. The stating of the caution does not automatically mean the statement was voluntary, nor does its absence mean that the statement was not voluntary. A videotape of the statement may help the court assess whether the statement was given voluntarily. One cannot emphasize enough the importance of good note-taking by security officers. Notes must include the verbatim conversation between the officer and the accused. Also, it might help prove voluntariness if the accused wrote the statement.

A secondary caution should be given if the accused must deal with more than one person in authority during the investigation. For example, once a police officer removes the accused from a private security officer, it is recommended that the police officer provide a secondary caution to ensure that the accused understands that whatever someone else in authority has said, there is no obligation to answer any questions.

If a statement by an accused is given to a person not in authority (such as a friend), a *voir dire* is not necessary, as the statement will be assumed to have been voluntarily given. This practice of confessing or bragging to friends and acquaintances can very easily be turned against the accused, since the inculpatory statements are assumed to be voluntarily given and therefore tend to be automatically admissible.

It is also wise practice for security personnel to provide the formal caution to a suspect who has not been arrested, where reasonable grounds exist that the suspect committed an offence. Even though the Charter may not apply in the situation at hand, any incriminating statement must still be given voluntarily.

Steps to a Citizen's Arrest

In light of the above information, the following is a general guideline when conducting citizen's arrests.

1. Identify yourself as security.
2. Make it clear that the person is under arrest (example: "You are under arrest.")
3. Simultaneously with steps 2 and 3, possibly touch or use reasonable force (lightly grasp the elbow) to demonstrate that you are physically in control of the accused.
4. Tell the person the reason for the arrest (s.10a).
5. Inform the person of their right to counsel (s. 10b).
6. Caution the accused in regard to statements.
7. Turn the person forthwith over to a police officer.
8. Record verbatim notes contemporaneously (soon afterward).

CIVIL LAW

Civil or private law (not to be confused with the civil system of law operating in Quebec) consists of rules governing the legal relationship between private individuals, between organizations, or between individuals and organizations. Civil law exists mainly to compensate individuals or organizations for wrongs done by other individuals or organizations. It is possible for a public case and a private case to arise from the same incident. Since the criminal case is almost always brought on by the state (usually by the Crown attorney), there is typically no personal compensation for the victim. However, private law allows for personal remedies, such as financial compensation, for harm or loss caused by others. In other words, society's interests are protected by the state, specifically by the Crown, who may prosecute even without the victim's consent in order to punish the offender on behalf of society. On the other hand, society has no interest in whether the victim decides to initiate a civil action to seek compensation. Contract law and tort law are the two areas of "purely" civil law (as opposed to the quasi-civil laws, such as the TPA and HTA). Both types are of importance to those working in private security.

Contract Law

Contract law is an agreement between two or more competent persons that imposes rights or duties on the parties involved. If there is a violation of the agreement that causes a member of the party to suffer losses, the party suffering the loss may initiate a civil action to remedy to the wrong (by seeking compensation). For example, if you buy a new radio from a retail store that later turns out to be damaged and unworkable, one of your options is to ask the retail store to replace the radio. If the store refuses to do this, you may sue under contract law for the value of the radio. Contracts may also be "expressed" or "implied." An express contract is one that has been clearly stated in words; an implied contract is based on actions, such as previous patterns of behaviour. An example of an express contract is when the security manager of a guard company enters into a specified arrangement in writing with a client to provide a number of personnel to perform specific services for a certain price. An example of an implied contract is a customer ordering food at a restaurant, the implication being that the person eating the food will pay for it before leaving.

David Ray (1993: 71) points out the following things for consideration when entering into a contract:

1. Whenever possible agreements should be in writing. Most provinces have a statute of frauds which stipulates that some agreements are not enforceable unless they are in writing:
   - those not completed within one year
   - those to make good the debt of another; and,
   - those relating to real property

2. Once an agreement is in writing it should only be changed in writing. The courts are reluctant to accept evidence of an oral change to a written document because if it was important enough to reduce to writing initially, any amendments should also be put down on paper.

3. A contract will not be enforceable if it is for an illegal purpose. For example if an investigator is hired to do illegal wiretaps the contract would not be enforced by the courts because it violates the Criminal Code.

Tort Law

Tort is defined as a civil wrong not covered by a contract that one person commits against another person or another person's property. Amirault and colleagues describe the law of torts and its origin as follows:

> The *law of torts* is the set of rules that has been established by the courts to apportion blame for such private wrongs and to determine the amount of compensation that should be paid by the person who has committed the wrong to the injured party. The word "tort" comes from the Norman French, in which it meant a "wrong." The French word itself derives from the Latin *tortus*, meaning "twisted." (Amirault et al., 1988: 72)

For instance, if Ivan takes his fist and assaults John by punching him in the face, there is most likely no contract governing this action. John cannot receive compensation under the law of contracts; rather, he must sue under the law of torts. In this situation a public case would likely arise in addition to the private tort lawsuit, since assault is also a criminal offence. Another example of a criminal case and a tort lawsuit arising from the same circumstances is the notorious O.J. Simpson case. Simpson was tried for homicide, and was acquitted; soon after, he was the defendant in a wrongful death tort lawsuit, in which he was found liable for the deaths of two people. This apparently contradictory result can occur for many reasons; typically, however, it is because the burden of proof in a criminal case is beyond a reasonable doubt (that is, to a moral certainty) whereas in a civil case it is based on a balance of probabilities (that is, is it more likely than not that the act was committed by the defendant).

There are two kinds of torts: intentional and negligence (or unintentional). An intentional tort is found in the example where Ivan intended to punch John in order to harm him. A negligent tort revolves around whether a person's conduct, however unintentionally, deviated from the conduct of a reasonable person. An example would be if the driver of a car was driving in excess of the speed limit while impaired by alcohol and inadvertently hit and broke the leg of a pedestrian who was walking on the sidewalk. This driver, in addition to any criminal charges, may very well be sued under a negligent tort, since his action clearly deviated from the conduct of a reasonable person and caused harm to another person.

Examples of tort lawsuits that may involve private security personnel are listed in Table 3.7.

TABLE 3.7   Tort Laws

TORT	DESCRIPTION
Assault	An intentional act that may cause a reasonable apprehension of physical harm in the mind of another (example: threatening someone to obey your demands).
Battery	The offensive contact of a person, either directly or indirectly, without consent (example: using excessive or unreasonable force).
False imprisonment	Unlawfully restraining someone so as to deny them freedom, through either physical or psychological means (example: security arresting someone without seeing the offence take place).
Fraud	Willfully making a false statement with the intent of having someone act on it and thereby suffer loss or harm (example: passing a cheque with knowledge of insufficient funds).
Intentional infliction of emotional distress	Willfully causing someone to suffer a severe emotional reaction (example: falsely accusing someone that they are going to be fired from work).
Conversion	Taking someone else's property without their permission (this is the civil counterpart to theft; example: stealing a radio from a store).
Negligence	Two components: "First, that a person is held to the standard of the reasonable person in the conduct of ordinary human affairs; and second, a person will be held responsible for any harm directly caused to others falling below this standard" (Amirault, 1988: 83) (examples of professional negligence: a security consultant incompetently provides advice that causes harm to the client; occupiers fail in their duty by not providing a reasonable amount of security to customers).
Defamation	Injuring a person's reputation by knowingly disseminating false information, either orally (which is slander) or in writing (which is libel) (example: falsely accusing someone of committing a crime).
Nuisance	The "act of wrongfully allowing or causing the escape of harmful or obnoxious things onto another person's land—for example, water, smoke, smell, fumes, gas, noise, heat, vibrations, and electricity that are capable of harming or destroying a person's health or property" (Amirault et al., 1988: 73) (example: knowingly failing to meet standards concerning dangerous chemical storage with the result that another person is harmed).
Malicious prosecution	Bringing forward a criminal action (arrest, prosecution) against a person with no basis and with malice aforethought (example: a security officer unlawfully arresting someone due solely to a strong personal dislike of the arrestee).

The purpose of bringing forward a tort lawsuit is to seek compensation for injury suffered. The courts award two broad types of damages: special and general. **Special damages** relate to quantifiable matters, such as lost income due to absence from work, and medical or repair expenses. **General damages** are awarded for those matters which are more difficult to assess, such as pain and suffering or future loss of business. Other remedies used in tort law include nominal and punitive damages. **Nominal damages** (also known as exemplary damages) refer to situations where small amounts of money (perhaps one dollar) are awarded to the plaintiffs, as an indication that they were right in principle but that they did not suffer significant loss requiring compensation. **Punitive damages** may be awarded to the plaintiff in addition to the above remedies in order to punish the defendant. As well, punitive damages are meant to deter the defendant (specific deterrence) and others (general deterrence) from committing a similar act in the future. Money is at issue in tort lawsuits rather than punishments such as incarceration, which are not an option in a civil trial. (Recall that the punitive damages assessed against O.J. Simpson were well over $10 million.)

Society is becoming more litigious. This is especially evident in the United States. Another reasonable assumption is that Canada is not far behind our neighbours to the south. Next are cited a few Canadian examples of the tort of false imprisonment involving private security personnel:

In *Yarmine v. Gustafson* (1989) 15 A.C.W.S. (3d) 455 (B.C. County Court), the plaintiff was mistakenly accused and arrested for shoplifting by a store employee, and received (general) damages for assault and wrongful imprisonment in the sum of $5000. In *Northcott v. Johnson et al.* (1982) 18 A.C.W.S. (2d) 238 (Ontario Small Claims Court), the plaintiff was arrested lawfully by a security chief under the Trespass to Property Act (Ont.). However, the security chief had no intention of turning the plaintiff over to the police for further prosecution. As a result, the plaintiff was subsequently awarded $500 in general damages. In another case, *Gilchrist v. Raymond Lee Pharmacy Ltd.* (1988) 11 A.C.W.S. (3d) 192 (Ontario High Court of Justice), the plaintiff was falsely imprisoned for one hour for apparently stealing a package of cigarillos. Here, despite there being no evidence of embarrassment or humiliation in the presence of friends, the plaintiff was awarded $2500 in general damages for the loss of liberty. In *Freeman v. West Vancouver (District)* (1991) 24 A.C.W.S. (3d) 936 (British Columbia Supreme Court), a security guard who serviced automated teller machines "was detained arbitrarily when he was mistakenly arrested and unnecessarily detained at [the] police station." The security guard was awarded general damages of $10 000 and punitive damages of $5000.

SUMMARY

There are many laws, both in statute and in common law form, that directly affect the actions of security personnel. The purpose of this chapter was to present some of these more relevant laws and to show how they apply to practical situations. This chapter outlined what security personnel should understand about the law before taking action against another individual. Discussed were the following:

- Criminal law
- Definition of arrest/detention
- Arrest authority under the Criminal Code/Trespass to Property Act/Highway Traffic Act
- Search authority

- Right to counsel and caution
- Civil liability

The information presented in this chapter should serve as a general guideline rather than a rulebook, and as a starting point for further discussion and debate. Unfortunately, there has not been much case law on arrest, detention, and search procedures that has dealt specifically with actions of private citizens, such as security personnel. And the cases that do exist concerning private security have not been fully addressed by the Supreme Court of Canada. Perhaps one day many of the legal issues discussed in this chapter will be clarified by the SCC.

The reader must be aware that the judicial guidelines for private security may well change in the future. For this reason, security personnel should take a proactive approach and seek clarification for their actions, not only from their employer but also from academic and jurisprudence research. We are living in an "information age" in which a large majority of the people can access information. By staying aware of recent case law, security officers can take a proactive stance. If they become involved with an organization whose security policy directives are unlawful, they will be able to protect themselves from liability. One does not automatically escape liability simply by stating, "I just followed the policy."

REVIEW QUESTIONS

1. Explain both common and civil law systems. Which system has a greater impact on Canadian laws?

2. Name five areas where our Constitution has allotted authority to the federal government, and five where it has allotted authority to the provincial governments. What specific areas in the Constitution have particular relevance to the private security industry?

3. (a) List five legal rights, and the Charter sections that refer to them.

    (b) Why is it that government can not violate the Charter of Rights and Freedoms?

4. Define criminal law and list five statutes that, if violated, are criminal offences. Explain how criminal law is classified, and the implications of this classification.

5. Describe the differences in powers of arrest under the Criminal Code between a private citizen and a peace officer.

6. Is the violation of a Trespass to Property Act considered a crime? Explain.

7. When may security personnel search an arrested person? Explain fully.

8. Explain fully sections 10(a) and 10(b) of the Charter in terms of how these conditions are satisfied subsequent to a citizen's arrest.

9. Is giving a caution a statutory requirement? Why is the caution given?

10. List the eight steps to an arrest mentioned in this chapter.

11. Explain contract and tort law, and give two examples of each where the laws could apply to the actions of private security personnel.

RISK MANAGEMENT/ ASSET PROTECTION

CHAPTER OBJECTIVES

- Identify and apply the five-step risk management approach.
- Understand how risk management fits into the overall security function.

Management can be defined as the planning, organizing, leading, and controlling of resources to meet objectives in a cost-effective manner. So, *risk management* involves managing risks so as to prevent or mitigate any loss to the organization. This chapter provides an overview of how a risk management approach can be used to protect assets in any environment. Risk management involves more than simply arranging appropriate insurance coverage against certain types of potential loss. It is an integral part of the overall security function.

FIVE-STEP PROCESS OF RISK MANAGEMENT

Risk management can be further defined as the managing of risks through a logical five-step process:

1. Identification and analysis of risk.
2. Examination of alternatives.
3. Selection of appropriate alternative(s).
4. Implementation.
5. On-going review.

1. Identification and Analysis of Risks

Assets

Involved here is the identification of assets that must be protected, such as property, products, equipment, money, personnel, and information. Approaches that aid in identifying assets at risk include security surveys and personal inspections. Specifically, these assets can be divided into four categories of potential loss:

Property loss	Involves loss to real and personal property.
	Real—Immovable property such as land and buildings.
	Personal—Movable property such as vehicles and computers.
Net income loss	Consists of a reduction in revenue or an increase in expenses due to a particular incident.
Liability loss	Involves the costs of lawsuits against an organization, such as negligence claims.
Personnel loss	Could involve the death, disability, retirement, resignation, or layoff of an individual that deprives the organization of his or her skills.

Risks

The risk exposure of these assets—that is, through theft, fire, earthquakes, and so on—must be determined. A list of all the exposures (or perils) an organization faces is impossible to provide here because each organization faces its own unique risks. For example, the main risk in a large paper warehouse is fire, whereas theft is probably the main exposure in an uptown jewellery store. Some useful tools for identifying risk or exposure are surveys, financial records, and relevant industry statistics. Below are listed some general causes of loss that an organization may encounter. Remember that these may overlap depending on the circumstances.

- Criminal actions, including theft, fraud, mischief, and bomb threats
- Industrial disaster, including fire, explosion, and chemical leak
- Natural disasters, including flooding, earthquake, and windstorm
- Employee error or actions, which include inaccurate accounting, negligent actions, absenteeism, substance abuse, and work stoppages and strikes
- Business interruption, which includes production stoppage, bankrupt supplier, decrease in market share, and loss of major customer

See Figure 4.1, which illustrates the relationship of risks and assets.

Probability

Once the assets and their exposures have been identified, the next stage is to calculate the probability that certain events will occur. This process is necessarily subjective, since event predictions are more art than science. Here again, industry statistics, historical records, and statistical software (example: earthquake risk assessment programs) may minimize the subjective component of probability determination. For example, retail store owners may refer

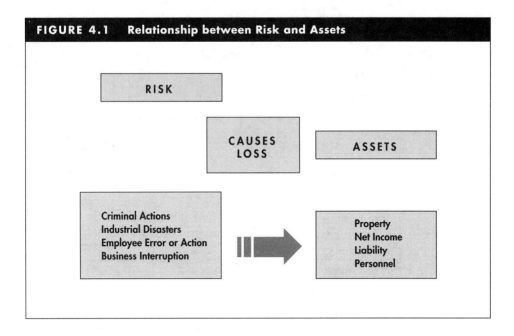

FIGURE 4.1   Relationship between Risk and Assets

to industrywide retail studies on theft when determining likely losses at their location. Historical internal records on theft, if properly maintained, may provide further insight, especially if surrounding conditions have not changed.

Probability can range from highly unlikely to virtually certain. For example, in a Manitoba retail store the probability that lower-priced items such as pens and candy will be stolen is very high; an earthquake at the same location would be classified as highly improbable.

Criticality

Criticality relates to the financial impact, usually measured in dollars, if a loss does occur. For example, there are likely to be a variety of costs if one computer is stolen:

- Replacement of computer (permanent and possibly temporary as well)
- Interruption of business
- Insurance deductible/premium
- Internal investigation
- Possible loss of confidential information
- Discounted cash (money lost when invested funds need to be withdrawn to pay costs)

In other cases of loss—such as injury to an employee, reduced morale, and loss of the organization's goodwill—criticality may be more difficult to quantify. Criticality may range from relatively unimportant to fatal (as in bankrupt). Thus, returning to the example of the Manitoba retail store, the theft of pens will likely have a minimal impact on survivability, while an earthquake, or a serious internal fraud (which is more likely), might be fatal to the continued existence of the organization.

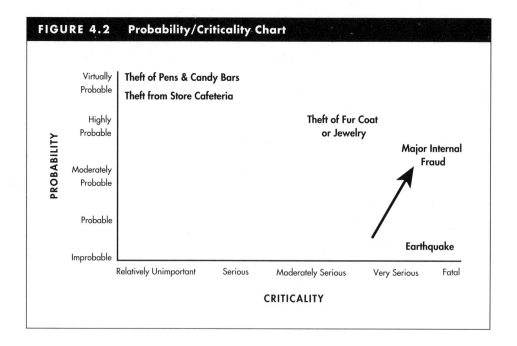

FIGURE 4.2   Probability/Criticality Chart

See Figure 4.2 for an idea as to where some events might be placed on a probability/criticality chart. Note that the closer an event falls toward the top right-hand corner of the chart, the more of a priority it is.

2. Examination of Alternatives

Two basic types of risk countermeasures are risk control and risk financing. Risk *control* is meant to minimize the probability and/or criticality of a loss; risk *financing* involves paying for losses once they occur.

Risk Control

Many risk control solutions involve the following countermeasures:

- Physical controls, which include fencing, gates, lighting, alarms, identification, video cameras, locks, architecture, landscaping, electronic access cards, and so on.
- Procedural controls, which include operating systems and procedures.
- Personnel controls, including employment screening.

There are seven basic types of risk control techniques (see Table 4.1).

Risk Financing Techniques

Risk financing involves generating funds to deal with losses when they occur. These funds could come from the company itself (a procedure known as retention) or from another organization such as an insurance company (a procedure known as transfer). Both risk

TABLE 4.1	Risk Response Options		
Technique	**Purpose**	**Example**	**Solution**
Risk elimination	• Eliminate loss	• Cheque fraud occurs	• Do not accept any more cheques
Loss prevention	• Reduce the probability of a certain loss	• Theft of clothing	• Place electronic alarm tag on clothing
Loss reduction	• Reduce the criticality of a certain loss	• Customer trips and falls while shopping	• Ensure proper first aid is administered
Segregation of loss (separation and duplication)	• Arrange resources, by either separating or duplicating them, so one event cannot cause loss to all resources	• Loss of computer information	• Separating (i.e., storing various information on different computers) • Duplicating (i.e., making backup copies)
Contractual transfer	• Transfer legal and financial responsibility for a loss	• Financial loss during bank deposit	• Hire armoured-vehicle company to transport cash
Risk acceptance	• Acknowledge the risk, but decide it's not cost effective to reduce it	• Theft of individually wrapped candies from a bin	• Accept this loss as the cost of doing business
Combination	Mitigate losses by combining the above techniques		

financing techniques are used to counter loss. For example, some types of loss cannot be commercially insured, or the premiums are too expensive; in such cases the retention approach must be taken.

3. Selection

Decisions as to which risk management strategy to use—risk control or financing, or both—depend largely on the following:

- Business objective during and after loss (remain stable, continue growth, legal considerations, and so on)
- Cost effectiveness of strategy
- Will the desired goal be met through this strategy?

4. Implementation of Appropriate Alternative(s)

Implementing a risk management strategy involves coordinating many resources. For example, installing video cameras in a retail store to prevent theft will likely require the commitment of a number of departmental employees in developing and adhering to policies. As well, there is a need for technical support when it comes to installing and servicing these devices—support that quite likely will come from outside the organization.

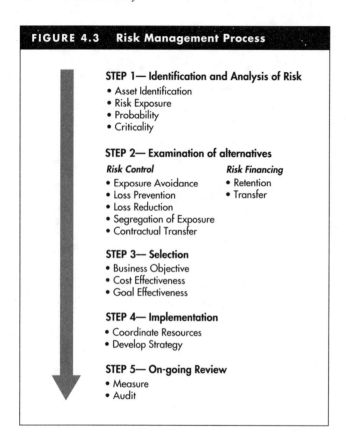

FIGURE 4.3   Risk Management Process

STEP 1— Identification and Analysis of Risk
• Asset Identification
• Risk Exposure
• Probability
• Criticality

STEP 2— Examination of alternatives

Risk Control
• Exposure Avoidance
• Loss Prevention
• Loss Reduction
• Segregation of Exposure
• Contractual Transfer

Risk Financing
• Retention
• Transfer

STEP 3— Selection
• Business Objective
• Cost Effectiveness
• Goal Effectiveness

STEP 4— Implementation
• Coordinate Resources
• Develop Strategy

STEP 5— On-going Review
• Measure
• Audit

5. On-going Review

After a risk management strategy is implemented, it is extremely important to continually measure its effectiveness, especially in light of changing circumstances. Any approach taken must have standards in place that can be properly measured, and corrected if needed. Audits are a useful tool in this review process. Figure 4.3 summarizes the five-step approach.

SUMMARY

This chapter provided a general understanding of risk management and how it fits into the overall security function. In many organizations, the roles of risk manager and security manager may be one and the same. If both positions do exist, they will have many common objectives, including the preventing or mitigating of loss of the organization's assets.

   The five steps involved in a risk management approach are as follows:

1. Identification and analysis.
2. Examination of alternatives.
3. Selection of appropriate alternative(s).
4. Implementation.
5. On-going review.

REVIEW QUESTIONS

1. What has been the traditional main task associated with risk management?

2. When identifying and analyzing risks, what are some useful tools for this process, and why are they useful?

3. Fully explain the terms *probability* and *criticality*.

4. What is the difference between risk control and risk financing?

5. What does an on-going review of a risk management program consist of, and why is it necessary?

OPPORTUNITIES

INDUSTRIES

Many companies exist solely to provide security services; many others provide for their own in-house security. For those who decide to start their own security service business, knowledge of specific industries is crucial to creating niches. Self-employment (which in this context means establishing one's own business) is certainly the trend in our economy. In fact, about 2.2 million Canadians—that is, 16 percent of the country's workers—now work for themselves

(*Report on Business*, June 1997: 44). However, as a general rule, in regard to the security sector, it is worthwhile (if not essential because of licensing requirements) to work for someone else before setting out on one's own. Keep in mind that many businesses fail as a result of improper planning and unsound business practices.

Most industries fall into one of the following categories, and require a certain amount of security. It is your responsibility to slot specific organizations in your area into these categories. Note that the industry referred to as "security" refers to contract security companies that solely provide security services. There are other companies for whom security, while integral, is not the main component; these other industries may utilize either in-house or contract security—or quite possibly both.

Educational
- Universities, colleges, high schools

Hospitality and entertainment
- Hotels, amusement centres, concerts, sports, casinos, bars, museums, theatres, restaurants

Financial
- Banks and trust companies, stockbrokers and regulators, credit/charge card companies

Government
- Federal, provincial, municipal

Health care/medical
- Hospitals, medical centres, nursing homes, colleges of physicians and surgeons, pharmaceuticals

Communications

- Telecommunications, cable, media, telephone, electronic services, broadcast

Manufacturing/industrial

- Automotive, textile, computers, aeronautical, apparels, chemical

Mining/forestry/petroleum

- Gas, oil, forestry, minerals

Public utilities

- Gas, hydro, water

Real estate

- Commercial, residential

Retail

- Department, grocery, clothing, electronic, discount, home centres

Security (contract security services)

- Private investigation, security guards, alarms, armoured car, consultants, locksmiths

Transportation

- Airline, rail, shipping, subway, streetcar, bus

SERVICES

Below is a list of activities that may come under the purview of private security personnel. The extent to which these activities are performed, and whether they are performed at all, depends on the organization and on the particular security position. Remember that some of these activities may very well overlap at times. Learn first what security services your targeted organization/market performs or requires. Then prove to the prospective employer either that you have successfully performed these services or that you have the potential to do so. If you have not performed these functions, you must be able to speak intelligently about what they entail and show that you are capable of learning what those functions require. The services listed below are mostly from the placement program brochure of the American Society of Industrial Security:

- access controls
- alarms
- anti-terrorism
- asset protection
- audits
- CCTV (closed circuit television)
- classified information
- computer programming
- computer security
- contingency planning
- crime prevention
- disaster management
- drug screening

- electronics
- employee screening
- executive protection
- facility security
- fire protection
- forensic accounting
- fraud investigations
- guard (in-house or contract)
- hazardous material handling
- intellectual property infringement
- intelligence gathering
- internal controls
- investigations

- labour relations
- litigation support/asset recovery
- loss prevention
- medical emergencies
- personnel administration
- physical security
- polygraph
- risk management
- safety
- security consulting
- surveillance
- surveys
- systems administration
- systems design
- technical engineering
- training
- warehouse/distribution

EDUCATION

An often asked question is this: What education is needed in today's security industry? The answer is that it depends on a variety of factors, including the organization you hope to work for, the security service you wish to provide, and your aspirations over the next several years. A good start is to ask those in your targeted organization about the education and experience needed to get hired. Some will undoubtedly tell you that experience is the most important asset and that a degree or diploma is secondary. This suggests that it does not matter where you learned certain skills, as long as you can apply them effectively. Other organizations place a great deal of importance on formal education.

Before entering any educational program, consider it carefully, even skeptically. Remember also that education is a lifelong process and that skills upgrading and keeping abreast of new findings is essential. Even if you are employed full-time, more and more courses are being offered for adults at night or through correspondence (which includes the Internet).

The following information is from *Canadian Security Sector: Training and Education*, a 1996 survey conducted by Joe Moylan and Raymond Pitre for the Industrial Adjustment Committee on the Security Sector. This information is meant as a general introduction to training and educational programs in the security industry. The list focuses on courses that are directly related to security in the "traditional sense"; not included are indirectly related courses such as computer science and business administration. Even so, remember that these latter two areas are becoming more essential for security professionals. Also left off the list are in-house training courses and professional development for in-house employees.

This list is divided into the following categories:

1. Regular credit programs.
2. Distance education/correspondence courses.
3. Private industry/security-related training (Western Canada).
4. Private industry/security-related training (Ontario).
5. Private industry/security-related training (Quebec and Eastern Canada).
6. Other accreditation programs.

The reader should be cautioned about the lack of standards in security-related education. Moylan and Pitre (1996: 3) found "that the variety of diplomas, certificates or statements of achievement obtained from students successfully completing the multitude of course[s] available today does not provide these graduates with a fair assessment of their worth in the market place nor does it give the employers a standard assessment by which to judge quality of programs."

A student attending an educational institution, whether it is private or public, should demand to know what has been done to provide a high quality of education at a reasonable price. For example, a student should ask careful questions about instructor qualifications and about co-op placements. A quality institution will keep good statistics and develop standards of quality that are carefully considered and closely monitored. Also: Do students evaluate instructors? If so, what happens to the evaluations? The institution should allow students, who are in fact customers and consumers, an avenue to provide systematic feedback. Programs must be continuously evaluated; performances must constantly be critically measured.

As a result of their survey, Moylan and Pitre made eight telling observations about the state of private security training and education:

- Professional relationships between the security industry and the providers of security training and education are weak at best.
- Training and education programs are operating in a void, with no relationship between institutions and industry.
- Very few graduates receive certification from national organizations upon graduation from their respective programs.
- Provincial legislation on security personnel that addresses issues of training, certification, and program accreditation is the exception rather than the rule
- There is no recent scholarly research addressing security issues.
- There is an absence of security-related programs at the university level.
- Research is impeded by the lack of a Canadian resource centre/clearing house on security matters.
- The RCMP and other similar governmental organizations may be important training sources for security-related courses.

Again, approach the following list as an overview of what training is available for the security field. When inquiring about these programs, apply some healthy skepticism.

Regular Credit Programs

English Courses

Canadian Studies and Criminology
- Simon Fraser University (B.C.)

Conservation Enforcement
- Lethbridge Community College (Alta.)

Conservation Enforcement Officer
- N.B.C.C. Miramichi (N.B.)

Correctional Officer Training
- Holland College (P.E.I.)

Correctional Services
- Grant MacEwan College (Alta.)

Correctional Services Work
- Cambrian College (Ont.)

Correctional Techniques
- John Abbott College (Que.)

Correctional Work
- Algonquin College (Ont.)
- Canadore College (Ont.)
- Centennial College (Ont.)
- Lambton College (Ont.)
- N.S.C.C. Hants (N.S.)
- St. Lawrence College (Ont.)
- Sault College (Ont.)
- Sheridan College (Ont.)
- Sir Sandford Fleming College (Ont.)

Corrections
- Mont Royal College (Alta.)

Corrections Academy
- Justice Institute of B.C.

Corrections Work
- S.I.A.S.T. Woodland (Alta.)

Court and Tribunal Administration
- Seneca College (Ont.)

Court Services Academy
- Justice Institute of B.C.

Crime and Deviance
- University of Toronto (Ont.)

Criminal Justice
- Camosun College (B.C.)
- Lethbridge Community College (Alta.)

- Open Learning Agency (B.C.)
- University College Fraser Valley (B.C.)
- V.C.C. Langara Campus (B.C.)
- Yukon College

Criminology

- College of New Caledonia (B.C.)
- Douglas College (B.C.)
- Kwantlen College (Surrey Campus) (B.C.)
- Mount Royal College (Alta.)
- St. Mary's University (N.S.)
- University of Ottawa (Ont.)
- University of Alberta
- University of Toronto (Ont.)
- University of Windsor (Ont.)
- Yukon College

Criminology and Criminal Justice

- Carleton University (Ont.)

Customs Administration

- Sir Sandford Fleming College (Ont.)

Fire Academy

- Justice Institute of B.C.

Fire Protection Engineering Technician

- Seneca College (Ont.)

Fire Protection Engineering Technology

- Seneca College (Ont.)

Fire Protection Technician

- Algonquin College (Ont.)

Human Justice

- University of Regina (Sask.)

Law

- Carleton University (Ont.)
- Dalhousie University (N.S.)

- Mount Allison University (N.B.)
- Queen's University (Ont.)
- University of Alberta
- University of British Columbia
- University of Calgary (Alta.)
- University of Manitoba
- University of Saskatchewan
- University of Toronto (Ont.)
- University of Windsor (Ont.)
- York University (Ont.)

Law and Justice
- Laurentian University (Sudbury Campus) (Ont.)

Law and Security
- Canadore College (Ont.)

Law and Security Administration
- Algonquin College (Ont.)
- Cambrian College (Ont.)
- Conestoga College (Doon Campus) (Ont.)
- Confederation College (Fort Frances) (Ont.)
- Confederation College (Thunder Bay) (Ont.)
- Durham College (Ont.)
- Georgian College (Owen Sound Campus) (Ont.)
- Humber College (Ont.)
- Lambton College (Ont.)
- Loyalist College (Ont.)
- Mohawk College (Ont.)
- Niagara College (Ont.)
- St. Clair College (South Campus) (Ont.)
- St. Lawrence College (Ont.)
- Sault College (Ont.)
- Sir Sandford Fleming College (Ont.)

Law and Security Administration (Customs Administration)
See Customs Administration

Law and Security Administration (General)
- Fanshawe College (Ont.)

Law and Security Training
- Holland College (P.E.I.)

Law and Society
- University of Calgary (Alta.)
- York University (Ont.)

Law Enforcement
- Mount Royal College (Alta.)
- Seneca College (Ont.)

Law Enforcement (Natural Resources)
- Sir Sandford Fleming College (Ont.)

Law Enforcement Administration
- University of Toronto (Ont.)

Law Enforcement and Security (Law Enforcement)
- Grant MacEwan College (Alta.)

Law Enforcement and Security (Security)
- Grant MacEwan College (Alta.)

Law Enforcement Career Preparation
- Keewatin Community College (Man.)

Law Enforcement Studies
- Carleton University (Ont.)

Law Office Administration
- Seneca College (Ont.)

Laws
- University of Manitoba (Man.)

Legal Administration
- Durham College (Ont.)

Legal Assistants
- Algonquin College (Ont.)
- Cambrian College (Ont.)
- Canadore College (Ont.)
- Capilano College (B.C.)

- Fanshawe College (Ont.)
- Grant MacEwan College (Alta.)
- Humber College (Ont.)
- Mohawk College (Ont.)
- Niagara College (Ont.)
- N.S.C.C. Cumberland (N.S.)
- Red Deer College (Alta.)
- St. Clair College (South Campus) (Ont.)
- St. Lawrence College (Ont.)
- Seneca College (Ont.)
- Sir Sandford Fleming College (Ont.)
- Southern Alberta (Alta.)

Legal Studies
- Carleton University (Ont.)
- University of Waterloo (Ont.)

Police Academy
- Justice Institute of B.C.

Police Education
- Fanshawe College (Ont.)
- Sheridan College (Ont.)
- Sir Sandford Fleming College (Ont.)

Police Science (Cadet)
- Holland College (P.E.I.)

Police Studies
- Memorial University (Nfld.)

Police Technology
- John Abbott College (Que.)

Retail/Industrial Security
- Lethbridge Community College (Alta.)
- N.S.C.C. Hants (N.S.)

Security Alarm Installing
- B.C.I.T. (B.C.)

Security and Alarm Systems Technician
- Algonquin College (Ont.)

Security Management
- Algonquin College (Ont.)

French Courses

Alphabetical list of regular/apprenticeship programs offered in French

Criminologie
- Université d'Ottawa (Ont.)
- Université de Montréal (Que.)

Droit
- Université d'Ottawa (Ont.)
- Université de Moncton (N.B.)
- Université de Sherbrooke (Que.)
- Université Laval (Que.)
- Université de Montréal (Que.)

Droit et justice
- Université Laurentian (Ont.)

Enquête
- Collège Ahuntsic (Que.)

Gestion appliquée à la police et à la sécurité
- Université de Montréal (Que.)

Gestion policière
- Université du Québec (Trois-Rivières) (Que.)

Intervention en délinquance
- Collège Ahuntsic (Que.)
- Collège de Maisonneuve (Que.)
- Collège F.X. Garneau (Que.)

Police et relations communautaires
- Collège Ahuntsic (Que.)

Réparation et dépannage de systèmes de sécurité

- C.S. Goéland (Que.)
- C.S. la Jeune Lorette (Que.)

Sécurité (installation et entretien)

- C.S. Goéland (Que.)

Services correctionnels

- Collège Boréal (Que.)
- Cité Collégiale (Ottawa) (Ont.)

Sûreté industrielle et commerciale

- Collège Ahuntsic (Que.)
- Collège de Drummondville (Que.)
- Collège de Maisonneuve (Que.)
- Collège F.X. Garneau (Que.)
- Collège de Sorel-Tracy (Que.)
- Collège St. Jean-sur-Richelieu (Que.)

Techniques correctionnelles

- N.B.C.C. Dieppe (N.B.)

Techniques policières

- Collège Ahuntsic (Que.)
- Collège d'Alma (Que.)
- Collège de l'Outaouais (Que.)
- Collège de Maisonneuve (Que.)
- Collège de Rimouski (CEGEP) (Que.)
- Collège de Sherbrooke (Que.)
- Collège de Trois-Rivières (Que.)
- Collège F.X. Garneau (Que.)

Techniques juridiques

- Collège Boréal (Que.)
- Collège Ahuntsic (Que.)
- Collège de l'Assomption (Que.)
- Collège F.X. Garneau (Que.)
- Séminaire de Sherbrooke (Que.)

Distance Education/Correspondence Courses (All Groups)

Athabasca University (Alta.)
- Legal Studies

Cabot College (Nfld.)
- Security Services

Carleton University (Ont.)
- Law Enforcement

Confederation College (Ont.)
- Security Administration

Elite Academy (Alta.)
- Private Investigation

Granton Institute (Ont.)
- Electronic Security
- Fire Sciences
- Firearms Repair and Maintenance
- Locksmithing
- Police Science

Humber College (Ont.)
- Security Services

ICS Canada (Que.)
- Police Science
- Private Investigation

Loyalist College (Ont.)
- Security Administration

Memorial University (Nfld.)
- Criminology

Mount Royal College (Alta.)
- Security Services

Niagara College (Ont.)
- Security Laws and Investigations Course (on-line)

Paul Paulson and Associates (B.C.)
- Security Services

Security Officer Career College Inc. (Alta.)
- Interior Protection Service
- Loss Prevention
- Personal Safety
- Private Investigation
- Security Services

Dalhousie University (N.S.)
- Police Leadership

University of Toronto (Ont.)
- Risk Management Certificate

Private Industry Security-Related Training (Western Canada)

Achieve Technology Ltd. (B.C.)
- Hazardous Material Management (TDG and WHMIS)

Business Training Institutes of Canada Inc. (B.C.)
- 700-hr Diploma Program (Security and Private Law Enforcement)
- Private Investigations
- Security Industry
- Retail Investigations

Canadian Crime Prevention Centre (Alta.)
- Social Security Issues
- Personal Safety
- Children Safety
- General Safety
- Industry Security

Canadian Investigation Academy (B.C.)
- Private Guard Security (basic to investigator level)

David L. Ray—Corporate Security Consulting Inc. (Alta.)
- Assets in the Workplace
- Managing Risk

- Detoxing the Workplace
- Security Law

Delorey Security and Defence Academy Inc. (B.C.)

- Security Patrol
- Executive Protection
- Lethal Force/Firearms
- High Risk Control Tactics

Edconserve (Associates) (B.C.)

- Police/Security Related Topics

Elite Academy of Investigative Training (Alta.)

- Security Related Course (Distance Learning)

Golden West Training Academy (B.C.)

- Investigations
- Computer Security
- Executive Protection
- General Security
- Specialty Seminars

G.R. Tech (B.C.)

- Security Alarm Installation Program

Hilltop Security Academy (B.C.)

- Security Personnel
- Basic Private Security
- Security Communication

ICS Canadian Limited (HQ: Que.)

- Police/Security Related Courses

Paul Paulson and Associates (B.C.)

- "The Professional Security Person" (Correspondence Course)

Robertson College Inc. (Man.)

- "Protection and Investigation Officer"

Security Communication International (B.C.)

- Security/Law Enforcement Related Courses

Security Officer Career College Inc. (Alta.)

- Guard Training
- Loss Prevention
- Private Investigation
- Protection Officer Training
- Self Defence

Security Training Academy International (B.C.)

- Basic Security
- Access Control
- Security Management
- Security Awareness Programs

Security Training Academy of Manitoba (Man.)

- Basic Security Officer
- Firearm Course
- Self Defence

The Firing Line (Man.)

- Basic Firearm Training Course
- Advanced Firearms Skills

Private Industry Security-Related Training (Ontario)

Academy for Private Investigators Canada Limited (Ont.)

- Street Surveillance
- Individual Assistance
- Evidence Gathering
- Insurance Fraud
- Court Appearance
- Testimony

Canadian Law Enforcement Learning Centre Inc. (Ont. & B.C.)

- Criminal Code
- Criminal Law
- Leadership/Management Conflict
- Personal Safety
- Loss Prevention

Canadian School of Private Investigation and Security (CSPI) (Ont.)
- Law/Law Enforcement
- Court Agent/Legal Assistant
- Private Investigation

Clarke Business College (Ont.)
- Law Clerk
- Business/Security Related Programs

Compass Security Consultants Inc. (CSCI) (Ont.)
- Security Personnel
- Physical Security
- Security Audits & Surveys
- Occupational Health & Safety
- Security Awareness
- Fire Protection
- Executive Protection
- Physical Security Systems

Elliot Goldstein (Ont.)
- Visual Evidence

International Security Associates (Ont.)
- Private Investigator Training
- Executive Protection
- Tactical Awareness and Survival
- Interview and Interrogation
- Kidnap and Hostage Survival
- Race Relations Awareness
- Personal Security
- Electronic Counter Measures
- Retail Investigation
- Personal Defensive Tactics
- Criminal Investigation
- Loss Prevention for the Small Business
- Security Officer Training

John N. Lance Security Training and Development Consultant (Ont.)
- Basic Security Officer Course
- Security Investigations Course
- Security Incident Commander Course

Lawson and Associates Limited (Ont.)

- Surveillance
- Accident Avoidance
- Investigative Interviewing
- Aboriginal Consultations
- Change
- Problem Solving
- Stress Management
- Time Management
- Team Building in Policing

McGraw-Hill Continuing Education Centre (Ont.)

- Specializes in technology area; correspondence courses

J. Moylan and Associates Security Services (Ont.)

- Security Guard Uniforms
- Security Supervisors Uniforms
- In-House/Specialty Courses
- Leadership and Management
- Crisis Intervention/Management
- Information Security
- Investigative Matter
- Security Law
- Personal Safety
- Basic Training (Can) CGSB—133.1–87

  [All aspects of the security function in government requirements]

O'Brian and Associates (Ont.)

- Loss Prevention
- Security Audit Programs
- Management Training

Ontario Business College (Ont.)

- Law Clerk
- Security Services

Ontario Guard Services (Ont.)

- Basic Security Guard Course
- Security Supervision

Scope Inc. (Ont.)

- Law Enforcement/Private Security
- Private Investigative Services
- Emergency Response
- Interview and Interrogation
- Surveillance Techniques
- Case Management and Report Writing
- Providing Executive Protection

Security Management Institute (Ont.)

- Investigative Interviewing
- Kinesics Interview Techniques
- Self-Defence Security/Law Enforcement
- Vital Techniques and Procedures
- Preparing for Disasters
- Statement Analysis

Private Industry Security-Related Training (Quebec & Eastern Canada)

Academy Canada (Nfld.)

- Corrections, Diploma Program
- Law and Security, Certificate Program
- Paralegal Studies, Diploma Program

Canadian Security and Consultants Ltd. (N.B.)

- Security Related Courses (range from basic to firearms training)

Centract College of Business Trades and Technology (Marystown) (Nfld.)

- Security Investigation
- Emergency Response

Centre de formation des professionnels en sécurité inc. (Green Field Park) (Que.)

- Ateliers de perfectionnement
- Formation sur mesure
- Technique de prévention et de sécurité
- Technique d'investigation

Collège national de sécurité (Que.)

- Arme à feu
- Détective privé
- Garde du corps
- Professionel en sécurité industrielle
- Tactiques de survie d'agents

Les Experts—Conseil FPC Inc. (Que.)

- Risk Assessment
- Safety Management
- Emergency Response

Les Experts–Conseil FPC Inc. (Montréal) (Que.)

- Gestion de la santé-sécurité
- Contrôle des pestes

T&R Goldshield Security Services Institute (Nfld.)

- Security Investigation
- Emergency Response

ICS Learning Systems (Que.)

Police Services

- Administration of Justice
- Patrol Procedures
- Criminal Investigations
- Surveillance and Investigating
- Collecting of Evidence
- Criminal Law/Criminal Code
- Investigation Procedures
- Traffic Accident Violations
- Enforcing Drug Controls
- Police Side Arms
- The Crime Lab

Private Security

- Introduction to Private Security
- Role of the Security Officer
- Private Security/Access Control

- Legal Powers
- Post Orders, Procedures and Patrols
- Criminal Investigations
- Interviewing and Report Writing
- Security Surveys
- Retail/Industrial Security
- Security in Special Settings

Wildlife Enforcement and Protection Studies (Nfld.)

- Diploma Program

Other Accreditation Programs

American Society of Industrial Security (A.S.I.S.)

- Certified Protection Professional (C.P.P.)

Association of Certified Fraud Examiners (C.F.E.)

- Certified Fraud Examiner (C.F.E.)

Canadian General Standards Board (C.G.S.B)

- Security guard and supervisor training

Canadian Society For Industrial Security (C.S.I.S.)

- Accredited Security Professional (A.S.P.)

International Foundation For Protection Officers (I.F.P.O.)

- Certified Protection Officer (C.P.O.)
- Certified Security Supervisor (C.S.S.)

RECOMMENDED EQUIPMENT/ACCESSORIES FOR JOB SEARCH

The following equipment and supplies are highly recommended for a career search campaign. One can mitigate the cost of such items by using other people's equipment when feasible; for example, many stores will send faxes for you, charging by the page.

- Laser printer
- Fax machine
- E-mail
- Internet

- Newspapers (local, *The Globe & Mail, Toronto Star*)
- Quality résumé paper (such as 24 lb. cotton, white or off-white)
- Quality envelopes
- Labels (preferably for laser printer; alternatively, if possible, put envelope through laser printer)
- Postage (either regular or priority)
- One quality black pen
- At least one quality interview outfit (preferably conservative)
- Telephone
- Answering machine or voice mail

INFORMATION SOURCES FOR AIDING JOB SEARCH

The tools listed in Table 5.1 are useful for obtaining information on organizations and industries. Many of these sources are available free in your local library.

TABLE 5.1 Information Sources	
SOURCES	**SPECIFIC INFORMATION**
Globe Information Sources	**The Guide to the Financial Services Industry** ($349) Provides background information primarily on Canadian public companies (revenues, executives, etc.). **Info Globe On-line** For a minimum of $70 per search, Globe staff will provide a custom search on specific companies within 24 hours of request (information includes financial matters, annual reports, media articles). Customers can do their own searches by accessing the on-line system via computer (cost: at least $100 per month for a minimum of 4 months) (1-800-268-9128).
Prospectus	Available when company becomes public (stock information, direction/strategy of company).
Annual reports	Available mainly from public companies, but may be obtained from private companies. Provide financial information and future direction.
Scotts Business Directory	Mostly manufacturing industry information, organized regionally and by Standard Industrial Classification (SIC). Available are directories, Selectory Profiler and Prospector, Product Line-Up, Ontario/Quebec and Western/Atlantic editions, Greater Toronto business editions, and distribution editions. Provides information on product, number of employees, square footage, revenues, executives. CD-ROMS available (1-800-668-2374).
Dun & Bradstreet Canada	Provides general company research (similar to Scotts) for manufacturing and service industries. Available are Canadian Key Business Directory, National Services Directory, Guide to Canadian Manufacturers, Regional Business Directory. Has products available on CD-ROM, and provides specific search capabilities by Dun & Bradstreet staff (1-800-668-1168).

SOURCES	SPECIFIC INFORMATION
Infomart Dialog	On-line information provider comprising over 450 databases and 330 million articles, abstracts, and citations. Can access on-line data bases individually via computer, or Infomart staff will conduct a search (1-800-334-2564).
Micromedia Limited	Information company that provides corporate and financial documents (Annual reports, prospectuses, etc.). Can access on-line databases individually via computer, or Micromedia staff will conduct search (1-800-387-2689).
Compact Disclosure	On-line service available at some libraries. Contains information on over 10 000 public and private companies in Canada and the U.S.
Canadian Business and Current Affairs	Periodical index that indicates where the company was mentioned (in the *Financial Post, The Globe and Mail, Maclean's,* etc).
CD-ROMS	Telephone directories (Canada and U.S.). Individual newspapers (including *Toronto Star, The Globe and Mail*). Also, see above sources (including Dun & Bradstreet).
Contacts/Networks/Associations	• American Society of Industrial Security (ASIS) • Association of Certified Fraud Examiners (CFE) • Canadian Alarm and Security Association (CANASA) • Canadian Society of Industrial Security (CSIS) • International Association of Special Investigation Units (Insurance) (IASIU) • International Foundation for Protection Officers (IFPO) • International Association of Insurance Fraud Agencies (IAIFA) • International Association of Auto Theft Investigators (IAATI) • Insurance Committee for Arson Control (ICAC) • Ontario Association of Chiefs of Police: Corporate Security Liaison Committee • Risk Management Consultants
Better Business Bureaus (BBB)	Find out in the last four years about types of complaints by customers (not by employees, however) about the organization, as well as how complaints were handled. Note: less than 5 percent of companies belong to the BBB.
Trade magazines	*Security Management, Canadian Security, Blue Line Magazine, Haute Protection*
Business magazines	*Financial Post, Report on Business, Canadian Business*
Newspapers	*The Globe and Mail, Toronto Star, (particularly the business sections), Financial Post,* etc.
Internet	See Internet sources listed in Table 5.2.

APPROACHES

This section deals mainly with approaches to seeking employment within organizations (as opposed to establishing one's own business, such as security consulting). There is often little real difference between establishing your own business and working on contract for another organization. The recent trend has been significantly toward contract work (as opposed to full-time employment).

Job search techniques vary greatly. Ask four people what they think of your résumé and you will probably get four different responses. When searching for work, seek advice from those around you, including friends, family, teachers, and security professionals. Think of this as a process of continuous improvement. Having heard all their advice, sift through it and discard any ideas that are not relevant to your own situation. Remember the old adage that a wise person is one who learns from others' mistakes.

There are basically three approaches to seeking careers in the security industry:

1. Responding to classified ads in the newspaper.
2. Search firms.
3. Contacting professionals for advice, including information on opportunities.

Responding to Advertisements

Most positions in the job market are not advertised in newspapers. This means that you must work harder to tap the non-advertised (or informal) market. This is especially true of jobs pertaining to security. Some estimates put the percentage of advertised jobs compared to the total job market at less than 10 percent. There are a number of reasons why all positions are not advertised. For example, companies requiring security expertise may not wish to expose to the public their need for security and the type of security expertise they require. To disclose either of these things might be to reveal a possible weakness. Also, an employer can expect hundreds of responses for an advertised position, and this makes the entire recruitment process rather costly and time consuming. In addition, some employers may not recognize their need for a security position; these will have to be "sold on the idea" by a prospective candidate. It would be a safe assumption that far fewer than 10 percent of jobs in the private security sector are advertised. All of this means that people looking for work in the security field are far less likely to do well in their job search if they restrict themselves to answering classified ads. You must keep checking the papers such as the *Toronto Star* and *The Globe and Mail*, if only to keep track of business trends; but you must also remember that these resources, as well as the Internet, will identify only a small percentage of available security positions.

Some Tips on Responding to Advertisements:

- Always find out to whom your résumé is being sent. Thus, if the ad says to send it to Human Resources, find out the name of the Director of Human Resources.
- Possibly, send a second résumé to the president or vice president or CEO of the company who is the ultimate decision maker. (You would have sent the first one to Human Resources.)
- Always include a one-page cover letter with your résumé, which should be no more than two pages.
- Try to use exact words from the job advertisement in your cover letter. Show how you meet/exceed the position's requirements. Your résumé will likely be discarded if it isn't clear that you meet the minimum requirements.
- Emphasize achievements. Do not simply list job descriptions. Employers want to see transferable skills, so make it easier for them to decipher your résumé.

- Use only the best paper (white or off-white).
- Laser-print every copy—that is, no mass photocopying.
- Each cover letter, and usually the résumé, must be customized to meet the needs of the particular employee. Your résumé will not be read if the cover letter does not attract the employer's interest. A final point: NO MASS MAILING.
- Make the cover letter and résumé as informative and "user friendly" as possible. That is, make it visually attractive—use bolding, shading, italics, underlining, capitalizing, and so on.
- Follow-up on the résumé within two weeks by telephone. If you are rejected, ask why (again seek advice).

Internet Advertised Job Sites

The Internet sites listed in Table 5.2 are worth checking regularly in the course of any job search. Be prepared to send an e-mail version of your résumé, which will be different from your traditional paper résumé, in that it will have fewer (or no) graphics, and no bolding, italics, underlines, and so on. I suggest a simpler résumé format for e-mail transmission because it creates fewer problems for addressees when they convert your résumé to their files. Never stop seeking advice on how to improve your résumé; stay aware of current résumé techniques by reading current literature and speaking with knowledgeable people.

Search Firms

Search firms (also known as headhunters) represent only a small part (less than 10 percent) of the overall job market. There are not many search firms that specialize in security-related positions. A few of the big accounting firms (such as Coopers & Lybrand and KPMG) are the exception; their executive search departments will place individuals in very high-end security positions, such as directors or managers of security.

It takes little effort to sign on with a search firm: often you need only to fax or mail in your résumé, which the firm will then keep in a database in the event a position becomes available. By all means use this approach, since there is nothing to lose; but also keep in mind that success rates for these firms tend to be low. Many recruiters have inside knowledge of certain industries/organizations. For example, they know it is usually not a good sign when a lot of employees are exiting a firm or "jumping ship."

Some Tips on Using Search Firms:

- Contact your local library for a directory of search firms in your province.
- Clearly explain to the recruiters what you are interested in doing; it is not their job to assess where you might fit in the industry.
- Follow up in person or by phone with the recruiter.
- A fax machine or e-mail will help you disseminate your résumé to as many recruiters as possible.
- Beware of firms that charge you a fee as opposed to charging the employer.

TABLE 5.2	Internet Job Search Sources

CANADIAN

Site	URL
Research on Canadian Companies	http://strategis.ic.gc.ca
Employment	http://ein.ccia.st-thomas.on.ca/agencies/cec
The Globe and Mail	http://www.theglobeandmail.com
Toronto Star	http://www.t-o.com
Canadian Jobs on the Internet	http://www.netjobs.com:8000/index.html
HEC Group (Ancaster)	http://hec-group.com
Ian Martin Ltd.	http://www.iml.com
Job Match	http://www.jcitech.com/jobmatch/
Job Hunt	http://www.job-hunt.org/
Career Networking	http://www.careerkey.com
CanWorkNet	http://canworknet.ingenia.com/canworknet
Canadian Job Source	http://www.irus.rri.uwo.ca/~jlaw/job_can.html
Cross-Canada Newspaper Job Classifieds	http://www.icom.ca/~willow/jobform.html
Résumé Canada	http://www.bconnex.net:80/~resume/mainmenu.htm

UNITED STATES

Site	URL
Career Path	http://www.careerpath.com
Career Mosaic	http://www.careermosaic.com
Job Center	http://www.jobcenter.com/team/emplinks.htm
ASIS (Security Related)	http://www.asisonline.org
Monster	http://www.monster.com
Recruitex	http://www.recruitex.com
Career Span	http://www.careerspan.com
Systems Net	http://www.systemsnet.com
Cweb	http://www.cweb.com
Job Bank	http://www.jobbankusa.com
Intelli Match	http://www.intellimatch.com
Career	http://www.career.com
Americasemployers	http://www.americasemployers.com
USAE	http://www.usae.com/~njs/
Career Magazine	http://www.careermag.com
Job Trak	http://www.jobtrak.com
Job Web	http://www.jobweb.com
OCC	http://www.occ.com
CareerExpo	http://www.careerexpo.com
CareerCity	http://www.careercity.com

Contacting Professionals

This approach is very lengthy, but likely the most rewarding. The concept is very simple: Talk to as many professionals in your area of interest as possible. Instead of asking them for a job, ask them for advice, including the names of other people to contact. You will not only learn more about the security industry and potential opportunities, but you will be building up a list of future contacts once you have found a security position.

This approach involves contacting people with a view to seeking their input on your specific situation. One method is to target an individual inside an organization that you would like to work for, and send that person a one-page letter that outlines your request for advice and summarizes your background and achievements. Be as specific as possible about what you hope to learn. This approach may work better than a "cold" telephone call, since the targeted person will have time to think about your request at their convenience, and will be holding a "hard copy" of your request. People by nature like to be asked for advice rather than be asked for a job, since there is less pressure; so make it clear that you are not pestering the targeted person for a job (even if this might in fact be the end result of your contact) and are only seeking an opinion and perhaps other names of people in the industry.

You should send one page only for two main reasons. First, if you send a standard résumé, many secretaries (who screen the mail) will automatically forward it to Human Resources, bypassing the decision maker. Second, it is obviously easier for someone with a busy schedule to read one page rather than two or three. When you only allow yourself one page to summarize your background and achievements, you are forcing yourself to be succinct and to the point. Think of your letter as an opportunity to present a mini-résumé.

Some Tips on Contacting Professionals:

- Your letter should contain the correct name, title, and address of the person from whom you are seeking advice. To find this information, look up company executives in the information sources listed earlier, such as Dun & Bradstreet Directory, or call the company directly (it is always a good idea to confirm a name you found in a directory).

- The first paragraph should state succinctly that you are seeking their advice (that is, not a job!) on how to better market yourself and search for opportunities within a specific field of security. You would like to meet them in person; as a last resort, you are willing to take this information over the phone.

- The middle paragraph should include a bullet list of your most important achievements (as many as you can fit in one page).

- The last paragraph should contain a specific date (or week) that you will call. This is usually three to four days after you think the person would have received your letter. Also, thank the person in advance for considering your request. (*You* make the call; don't wait for it.)

- If a secretary asks why you are calling, mention that the person you are seeking to speak with is expecting your call. After all, you mentioned on your one-page letter that you would be calling.

- Be able to summarize your background and achievements and to explain the purpose of your call within ten to fifteen seconds.

- Push for a face-to-face meeting.

- Push for other names and resources to help you become further informed. If applicable, mention who referred you to the person with whom you are presently speaking.

- Treat every telephone conversation and face-to-face meeting as an interview (after all, you are *always* being evaluated). Think about this in regard to matters such as your answering-machine message, telephone mannerisms, and correspondence, and your appearance/clothes when meeting someone in person. Invest in a quality business outfit, preferably a conservative one.

- Always send out thank you letters after meeting with someone, and usually even after speaking to someone over the telephone. One can never be too courteous, and sending a thank you note takes little time.

SUMMARY

Any person searching for a career in security must have a focused strategy that includes answering the following questions:

- What industries are you targeting, and why?
- What security services do the targeted organizations require, and how can you provide them?
- What are you doing to constantly upgrade your skills?
- Once you have targeted an organization, how do you approach the decision maker?
- How do you research the targeted organization?

Too many people go to potential employers and expect jobs, as opposed to clearly telling the decision maker how the organization can benefit from your expertise. Sometimes, you must persuade the decision maker that if the position does not exist, then perhaps it should be created. Finding the right position may very well take you several months from the initial point of contact to an actual job offer.

REVIEW QUESTIONS

1. Identify industries that require security services. List specific organizations in your area that fall into these categories. What security activities occur (or at least should occur) within these organizations?
2. List twenty security activities that might be performed in a large multinational corporation.
3. What are some problems with security-related education and training?
4. What equipment and accessories are recommended for a job search?
5. List ten information sources available when researching a specific organization or industry.
6. Should you spend the bulk of job search time responding to advertised positions? Explain.
7. Why might organizations not want to advertise security positions?
8. What does it mean to seek advice (as opposed to a job)?
9. List five organizations or associations that you can belong to in order to network and become more informed about various security-related topics and opportunities.

FURTHER RESEARCH

CHAPTER OBJECTIVE

In this chapter I will provide the reader with more tools for researching the private security industry in Canada. First I will review the academic literature about private security in Canada. Then I will list various Internet sites that are police/security related. I hope readers will find this information useful in career planning.

ACADEMIC LITERATURE

This literature review is taken mostly from my work for Ontario's Solicitor General (1995) and concentrates on academic material about private security in Canada. The United States and United Kingdom are also touched on.

There is little current research being done about the Canadian private security industry. Whatever research has been done in this country was done from the mid-1970s to early 1980s. In the United States, several large-scale studies were conducted between the early 1970s and 1990. Unfortunately, there are difficulties applying American data to the Canadian context because the laws and practices are different.

Most Canadian research was conducted under the auspices of the University of Toronto's Centre of Criminology. The main authors of this research were Philip C. Stenning and Clifford D. Shearing. They and their colleagues provided a solid foundation of academic research into private security; unfortunately, there has been no follow-up.

Before Stenning and Shearing, most of the published work about private policing in Canada was found in police and security trade journals, was largely descriptive in nature, and was written from an industry perspective (Trofymowych, 1992: 15). The first American study that examined private security was conducted by James Kakalik and Sorrel Wildhorn for the Rand Corporation (Kakalik and Wildhorn, 1971). This study, known as the "Rand Report" consisted of five volumes and reported on the size of the industry, and on the trends within it, with an emphasis on contractual security. The most notable finding in this report was that the "average security guard" was an older man with little education and training who was poorly paid. The following year, private security was examined in the United Kingdom (McClintock and Wiles, 1972). Both above-mentioned studies documented the rapid growth of private security, and emphasized that private security personnel would soon surpass the public police in number, if they had not already done so. These studies helped rekindle interest in this subject in Canada; presumably this led the Toronto Centre of Criminology to develop a research plan.

Canadian research began in 1973, with a workshop on Private Policing and Security in Canada. This workshop was convened to discuss issues of common concern to stakeholders, and to determine future areas of research. Fern Jefferies prepared an annotated bibliography, *Private Policing: A Bibliography*, which relied heavily on American sources. This reflected the lack of Canadian data at the time. Another document compiled by the Centre of Criminology, *Private Policing and Security in Canada: Selected Readings for a Workshop*, contained selected articles and reports, which were distributed to participants. This document contained some of the current research and thoughts on private security that corresponded with the workshop agenda. In 1974 a further document, *Private Policing and Security in Canada: A Workshop*, reported on discussions in the workshop, including future research needs. Some of the research needs identified were these: to determine the number of people employed in the industry, and what tasks they performed, and what controls were or should be placed on them in terms of regulation.

Next, the staff at the Toronto Centre of Criminology developed a research plan in response to the workshop results. The first report, *The Legal Regulation and Control of Private Security in Canada (A Working Paper)* (Stenning and Cornish, 1975), was a summer research project that provided a preliminary overview of legal controls and regulation of private security in Canada.

In 1977, three reports were produced by the Toronto Centre of Criminology. The first was produced by Farnell and Shearing and was titled *Private Security: An Examination of Canadian Statistics, 1961–1971*. This report examined "the security industry in Canada on a national basis by providing an analysis of publicly available statistical data on the industry" between 1961 and 1971 (Farnell and Shearing, 1977: xiv). Unfortunately, as the report itself cautioned, much of the information was of a secondary type, and the authors had to extrapolate from it for their study. Thus, some of the findings were disputable.

The second report, *Private Security, Police and the Law in Canada* (Freedman and Stenning, 1977), was also produced in 1977. The authors reviewed and analyzed both federal and provincial legislation regulating or encroaching upon private security in Canada. Their results included the finding that the "private security industry ... remains virtually unrecognised in Canadian statutory and case law" (Freedman and Stenning, 257).

The last report produced in 1977 was *Private Policing: An Examination of In-House Security Operations*, by Fern Jefferies. Her mandate was to collect quantitative data on the number of in-house security personnel and security operations and to categorize and define these security functions. Her sample consisted of 21 commercial organizations and 231 security personnel. The structures of the various organizations were also examined. Some key findings of this study were as follows: average age of respondents was 45.2 years; 13.4 percent of respondents were women; 35.5 percent of the sample had no high school education; 12.99 percent of the sample had attended university; and 16.9 percent had taken courses at community college.

In 1979, Shearing and Stenning wrote *Search and Seizure: Powers of Private Security Personnel*. These authors examined the legal authority of private security personnel by researching and interpreting much of the relevant case law that existed at the time. Obviously, the reader must keep in mind that the book was written before the Charter of Rights and Freedoms was enacted in 1982 and that therefore many reported judicial decisions may have changed significantly.

A 1980 report from the Toronto Centre of Criminology about private security, *Contract Security in Ontario* (Shearing, Farnell, and Stenning), ended the initial research program into private security. This report, which was more extensive than Fern Jefferies' study, looked at the licensed contract security industry in terms of agencies and people employed as security guards and private investigators. In total, 92 agencies and 392 security personnel participated in this study, which used surveys and interviews. Its key finding was that private security personnel act primarily within a "private justice" system as opposed to the public criminal justice system. In other words, if an employee is caught stealing, private security personnel are more concerned about profits and may simply issue a suspension, rather than involve the police and have the person prosecuted on behalf of the state.

Stenning and Shearing continued to publish work on private security independent of the Toronto Centre of Criminology. Stenning produced a report for the federal Solicitor General, *Firearms and The Private Security Industry in Canada*. In it he found that firearm use within the private security industry was very small; even so, he made several recommendations with respect to firearms administration. In a 1982 report, *Private Security and Private Justice: The Challenge of the 80s*, Shearing and Stenning described the development of private security and attempted to respond to some ethical and political questions that will confront governments.

Other work by Shearing and Stenning considers subjects such as "the nature and development of private security in Canada (1980), the growth and implications of modern private security (1981) ... the contribution of private security to modern policing (1982), and the implication of private security for social control (1983)" (Trofymowych, 1992: 17). The two did some further research in 1985 with Susan Addario regarding police, public, and corporate perceptions of private security. In 1987 Shearing and Stenning edited *Private Policing*, which contained essays by Canadian, American, and British authors that examined various issues in private policing and raised many questions regarding topics such as civil liberties, privacy, and social control.

In 1979 the Home Office in London produced *The Private Security Industry: A Discussion Paper*. This paper was designed to examine the background of private security, including definitions and numbers of security personnel. As well, the issue of self-regulation versus government regulation was discussed. The purpose of this document was to encourage discussion rather than make recommendations.

In the United States there have been four national studies in the past two decades that have examined private security: those conducted by the Private Security Advisory Council (1972–77), the Private Security Task Force (1975–76), and Hallcrest Systems, Inc. (1980–83 and 1989–90). Because there has been little Canadian research into private security, information from the above studies is often cited in the Canadian literature.

In 1988, consultant M. Kimberley completed a study of the private security industry in Newfoundland, *Security —Newfoundland and Labrador: Perspectives for the 1990s*, that was initiated by the Newfoundland Security Guards and Private Investigators Agencies Association. This study included a review of policies, legislation, and regulations affecting members of the industry, both licensed and unlicensed. Recommendations were made that included changes to the association, as well as to private security legislation.

In 1989, OPP Detective Sergeant D.A. Robbins wrote a paper, *Report to the Strategic Planning Committee on the Private Security Industry in Ontario*. The objective of this paper was to develop a strategic plan for dealing with the challenges and issues facing the private security industry in Ontario. Some of the more notable recommendations were that members of the Canadian Corps of Commissionaires and the in-house security industry be regulated, and that some minimum training be required for security guards. Also in 1989, Kenneth N. Smith and Robert J. Prouse wrote the *Canadian Private Security Manual*. These authors provided more practical information about private security from a uniquely Canadian perspective. Topics included contract/in-house security, management, legal authority, and various specific security operations (such as surveillance, transportation, and handling of dangerous goods).

In 1992 an unpublished report was written for the federal Solicitor General titled *Private Policing in Canada: A Review* (Trofymowych, 1992). This report outlined what had already been written about private security in Canada and pointed out areas where further research would be needed. Topics of research for the future included the following: number of individuals employed in private policing in Canada; number of companies providing private policing; number of individuals following standards set by the Canadian General Standards Board (CGSB) or the Canadian Society of Industrial Security (CSIS); specific type of work performed by private police; and the demographics of individuals working in private policing.

At about the same time as Trofymowych's report was completed, the Angus Reid Group wrote another report, *Law Enforcement and Private Security: A Public Perspective*, for the Canadian Society for Industrial Security. This report, also known as the Chapman Report, sought to identify attitudes toward private security among the legal and police communities as well as the Canadian public. Some of its notable findings were that 79 percent of Canadians encountered private security in their daily lives and that two-thirds felt that private security personnel were somewhat or very effective in carrying out their duties. Also, 58 percent of Canadians felt that private security should assume some traditional police duties where Criminal Code offences were not involved; but only 40 percent of lawyers thought so, and 24 percent of police. Half of those who thought private security should not be involved in police duties were opposed because private personnel were inadequately trained.

In 1993, Bonnie Erickson produced two reports that examined the Toronto security industry in terms of companies and employees with respect to the contract guard, hardware, and investigation categories. These reports were titled *Companies in the Toronto Private Contract Security Industry* and *People in the Toronto Private Contract Security Industry*. To determine the people and companies involved and the types of work performed in the private security industry, she sent questionnaires to 350 companies, and conducted interviews with 393 persons (155 employees, 46 supervisors, 70 managers, and 112 owners). Some notable findings: 80 to 90 percent of respondents had a high school diploma; 75 percent of the sample reported having some type of training; 50 percent of these rated their training as satisfactory. Many respondents favoured government control of agency standards.

Also in 1993 a study titled *Report on the Regulation of Private Security Industry in British Columbia* was produced for the Commission of Inquiry into Policing in British Columbia, headed by Justice Wallace Oppal (Mollard, MacKay, and Taylor). The authors focused on issues facing the security guard, private investigator, and armoured car industries in British Columbia. This report provided most of the background information that aided the commission when it produced the portions of the final 1994 document that dealt with private security. Several recommendations were contained in this document, titled *Closing The Gap—Policing and The Community: The Report (Vol. 2).* This document recommended regulating in-house security, Canadian Corps of Commissionaires, and armoured car personnel. It also recommended that there be minimum legislated training standards for private security.

David L. Ray wrote two books, *Canadian Private Security Law* (1993) and *Canadian Private Security: Administration* (1995). The former provides an excellent overview of the various public and private laws that affect the actions of private security personnel, including key federal and provincial statutes and some rules of evidence. The latter book, published in 1995, functions as a security manual and offers a more "how to" approach. Topics discussed include risk analysis, integrated protection programs, loss reporting, managing, safety and the environment, strikes and demonstrations, code of ethics, training programs, security policy, and contingency and strike planning.

The Canadian Centre for Justice Statistics produced a report in 1994 titled *Private Security and Public Policing in Canada*. This document examined the growth and personnel of private security and public police forces between 1971 and 1991. It was the first in-depth review by government of private security in Canada. Some findings of this study were that private security forces were growing faster than public police forces, and that private security outnumbered public police by slightly more than two to one. However, because of difficulties with definitions, these results are disputable. For instance, corrections officers were included in the "security guard and related security personnel" category, and some quasi-police personnel (such as railway transportation guards) were included under "private investigators." As well, it appears that only those who had full peace-officer status were included as members of the "public police personnel" category; thus, many other people that have law enforcement powers were excluded.

In 1994, John O'Grady Consulting, in collaboration with Radford Game and Associates, prepared a report titled *Occupational Standards and Training Needs Analysis* for the Canadian Security Union's Industry Training Advisory–Industrial Adjustment Service Committee. The purpose of this report was to recommend occupational and training standards for security guards. Recommendations were based mainly on the following: surveys of the Canadian Security Union (CSU) membership (1130 responses); survey/interviews of employers with whom CSU had collective agreements; focus groups with CSU members; interviews with clients; and reviews of other studies and standards. The report established occupational standards for security guards, including a five-week course; these were then compared to the requirements found in the Canadian General Standard Board (CGSB). Additionally, the security guard function was divided into three separate levels, ranging from watchperson to a quasi-policing role.

In 1995, Robert Gerden wrote a report titled *Private Security Review* for the Ministry of the Solicitor General and Correctional Services. The main purpose of this report was to pull together existing Canadian information on practices/issues concerning private security, and to briefly compare this information with that from other jurisdictions, such as the United States and the United Kingdom. Also in 1995, a report titled *Case Law for Security Management Selected Offences (1&2)* was produced by three Algonquin College students: Jack Hannah, Olav E. Ebrahim, and Dave Myles. This report considered specific case law subjects including arrest, search and seizure, occupiers' liability, and trespass. Also in 1995, Mike Lum prepared a report for the Aerospace and Defence Branch of Industry Canada, *Market Segment Analysis: Security Products.* This report focused on the manufacturing of defence security products and high-end private security products. Specifically, the following topics were examined: segment definition, global market, global supply, and international competitors. It was found that some of the major problems and issues facing this industry were the following: systems integration, industry fragmentation, research and development, technology transfer, export marketing, automated production, productivity, and the need for a forum to discuss common problems.

In 1996, D. James Hawkins and Elaine Z. Konstan wrote *The Canadian Private Investigator's Manual.* This manual presents an overview of investigative techniques and laws. Though it focuses on private investigators, this manual is applicable to many types of investigations. Topics covered include report writing, interview strategies, surveillance, and legal procedures. This book is one of the first in Canada to deal specifically with private investigators.

Also in 1996, three reports were conducted for the Industrial Adjustment Committee (IAS) on the Security Sector. Two of the three reports were compiled by Christopher Leclair and Stephen Long: *The Canadian Security Sector: An Overview* and *The Canadian Security Sector: Standards*. The former report identified the components of Canada's security industry and the broader security sector. Trends and issues were identified; key among them was the need to better assess the regulatory system, training, and standards in light of the projected growth of private security. The second report dealt mainly with identifying Canadian standards applicable to the security sector; but it also examined standards in the United States and United Kingdom. Many of these standards—most of them covering the hardware sector—were considered voluntary and thus were inconsistently applied. Also, surveys were sent to employers and employees of security companies in Canada. It was found that 76 percent of employers felt that there were insufficient standards in the security industry and that 72.6 percent felt that both government and the industry should be responsible for establishing higher standards.

The third report in this 1996 series to the IAS, *The Canadian Security Sector: Training & Education*, was produced by Joe Moylan and Raymond Pitre. This report "attempts to identify the scope of criminal justice and security related education and training in Canada." These authors essentially catalogued training programs from the following sources:

- University courses and programs
- Community college courses and programs
- Career college courses and programs
- Programs and courses offered by private firms and companies
- Distance education courses and programs at all levels

- Native justice programs and courses
- Government-sponsored co-operative programs
- Accreditation and certification organizations
- Police training centres
- Government training initiatives

There is a serious void in private security related literature in Canada. Simply filling this void with imported American research is not without its problems. Some of these problems involve the inherent differences between the United States and Canada in regard to laws, practices, and culture.

POLICE/SECURITY RELATED INFORMATION FROM INTERNET

The Internet list in Table 6.1 was prepared mainly by the staff at the Canadian Police College Library. It is meant to provide the reader with a variety of information sources that they may find helpful in the course of a security function. Keep in mind that as well, a variety of on-line services are available that—typically for a fee—will provide a wealth of information; these services include Infomart, Info Globe, Dun & Bradstreet, Scotts, and Micromedia. See Chapter 5 for more information on these on-line services. Finally, the reader should be aware that these sites may move around over time.

TABLE 6.1 Police/Security Internet Sites

SITE	URL
POLICE SITES	
COPNet & Police Resource List	http://www.cop.net/
Cplnet Home Page	http://www.cpinet.org/
Canadian Police Home Pages–HPD	http://www.atcon.com/HPD/other/cancop.html
The Police Pages	http://mcs.com/~jra/police/index.html
Law Enforcement Agencies on the Web	http://www.mcs.com/~crimdo/police.html
Law Enforcement Sites on the Web	http://www.ih2000.net/ira/ira.htm
Law Enforcement Links	http://www.leolinks.com/
The Police Officer's Internet Directory	http://www.officer.com/
Newsgroup:alt.law-enforcement	news:alt.law-enforcement
US Investigatory and Law Enforcement Offs.	http://gopher.usdoj.gov/bureaus/bureaus.html
UK Police Index	http://www.open.gov.uk/index/fipolice.htm
Specific Police Services	
Canadian Police College	http://www.cpc.gc.ca/
Collège canadien de police	http://www.ccp.gc.ca/
Welcome to the RCMP/Bienvenue à la GRC	http://www.rcmp-grc.gc.ca/

SITE	URL
The Official RCMP Centennial Museum Home Page	http://www.trakkerinc.com/rcmp/rcmphome.htm
RCMP Honour Roll	http://www.district.north-van.bc.ca/home/R_roll.html
Ontario Provincial Police Home Page	http://www.gov.on.ca/opp/
Metropolitan Toronto Police Service	http://www.metrotor.on.ca/services/abc/police.html
Ottawa-Carleton Regional Police Service	http://www.rmoc.on.ca/OCRP/home.htm
Halton Regional Police Service	http://www.worldchat.com/hrp/
Guelph Police Service	http://www.police.guelph.on.ca
Halifax Police Department	http://www.atcon.com/HPD/hpd.htm
Lethbridge Police Service	http://upanet.uleth.ca/~cottingham/
Niagara Regional Police Service	http://www.niagara.com:80/~nrpsweb
Winnipeg Police Services	http://www.freenet.mb.ca/iphome/w/wps/index.html
York Regional Police	http://www.flexnet.com/~yrp
Federal Bureau of Investigation–Home Page	http://www.fbi.gov/
Central Intelligence Agency Home Page	http://www.odci.gov/cia/
Chicago–CAPS Home Page	http://www.ci.chi.il.us:80/CommunityPolicing/
Metro-Dade Police Department Crime Lab Home Page	http://www.mdpd.metro-dade.com/crimelab.html
LRPD Special Investigations Division	http://www.storefront-usa.com/lrpd/specinv.htm

Crime Prevention

Crime Prevention	http://www.bconnex.net/~cspcc/crime_prevention/
Canada's National Crime Prevention Council	http://www.web.net/~ncpc/welcome.htm
International Centre for the Prevention of Crime	http://www.crime-prevention.org/icpc/
the Stolen Web Page	http://www.tshooters.com/stolen/stolen.htm
Greater Victoria Crime Stoppers: Home Page	http://vvv.com:80/crimestop
Joyce Street Crime Prevention Office	http://www.cutter.harbour.com/crimprev/index.html
NWPA Crime Prevention Office Home Page	http://www.harbour.com/crimprev/nw-police-cpo/
Crime Prevention Bookshelf	http://www.peelpolice.gov/cpbook.html

Forensics

Canadian Society of Forensic Science	http://home.istar.ca/~csfs/
American College of Forensic Examiners	http://www.acfe.com/
Zeno's forensic page	http://www.bart.n1/~geradts/forensic.html
Crime Scene Investigation	http://police2.ucr.edu/csi.htm

Crime Information

Wiretap Online Library–Questionables	gopher://wiretap.spies.com:70/11/Library/Untech
Guide to Lock Picking	http://www.lysator.liu.se/mit-guide/mit-guide.html
The Speed Trap Registry	http://www.nashville.net/speedtrap/

SITE	URL

Other Police/Security Related Sites

Coptalk IRC HomePage	http://www.chickasaw.com/~waedens/index.html
Partners Off Duty	http://www.murlin.com/~webfx/PartnersOffDuty/
NCSA–National Computer Security Assoc.	http://www.ncsa.com/
RSA Homepage	http://www.rsa.com/
CSIS–Canadian Security Intelligence Service	http://www.csis-scrs.gc.ca
Communications Security Establishment (CSE)	http://www.cse.dnd.ca
National High Tech. Crime Inv. Assoc.	http://www.sna.com/htcia/
Swedish National Police College: The Library	http://www.police.se/gemensam/phs/bibl_e.htm
Northwestern University Traffic Institute Home Page	http://www.nwu.edu/traffic/
The World's Most Wanted	http://www.mostwanted.com/
International Fugitive Lookout	http://www.usdoj.gov/criminal/oiafug/page1.htm
Police Dog HomePages	http://www.best.com/~policek9/k9home.htm
Spy vs. Spy–The Spy Store	http://www.SPYvsSPY.bc.ca/SPYvsSPY/
Overlord–Special Forces Home Page	http://www.spots.ab.ca/~overlord/
Stolen Web Page (list of missing or stolen property)	http://www.rtt.ab.ca/rtt/personal/stolen.htm
CIA World Factbook	gopher://marvel.loc.gov:70/11/federal/fedinfo/byagency/executive/cia
FBI Law Enforcement Bulletin	http://www.fbi.gov/leb/leb.htm
Emergency Preparedness Information eXchange	http://hoshi.cic.sfu.ca/~anderson
Safety Related Internet Resources	http://www.sas.ab.ca/biz/christie/safelist.html
Law Enforcement Product News	http://www.law-enforcement.com/
Law Enforcement and Private Investigation	http://netaccess.on.ca/~photobyt/law.htm
Bodyguard Home Page	http://www.iapps.org/

CRIMINAL JUSTICE AND LAW SITES

CJ Links	http://cjwww.csustan.edu/cj/rframe.html
Centre de recherche en droit public (CRDP)	http://www.droit.umontreal.ca/
Guide to Internet Resources in Criminal Law and Criminal Justice	http://www.law.ubc.ca/centres/icclr/icclr/guide/guide.html
Justice Information Center (NCJRS)	http://www.ncjrs.org/
Supreme Court of Canada	http://www.droit.umontreal.ca/opengov/s-courtf/sc.home.html
Canadian Law Resources on the Internet	http://mindlink.net/drew_jackson/mdj.html
FedWorld Home Page	http://www.fedworld.gov/

SITE	URL
Criminal Codes	
The Criminal Code of Canada	http://www.insight.mcmaster.ca/org/efc/pages/law/cc/cc.html
Code Civil du Québec–Table des matières	http://www.droit.umontreal.ca/cgi-bin/ccfTDM
Criminal Justice Organizations	
National Criminal Justice Reference Service	http://www.ncjrs.org/
NCJRS Gopher	gopher://ncjrs.org:71/11/
Int'l Centre for Criminal Law Reform and Criminal Justice Policy	http://www.law.ubc.ca/centres/icclr/index.html
International Criminal Justice Online	http://www.acsp.uic.edu/index.htm
UNCJIN Gopher	gopher://albany.edu.:70/11/newman/
United Nations Crime and Justice Information Network	http://www.ifs.univie.ac.at/uncjin/mosaic/
UNOJUST English Language Home Page	http://www.ncjrs.org/unojust/
UNO-Criminal Justice and Crime Prevention	http://www.ifs.univie.ac.at./~pr2gql/uno
Dept. of Justice/Ministère de la Justice (Canada)	http://www.canada.justice.gc.ca/
United States Department of Justice Home Page	http://www.justice2.usdoj.gov/
U.S. Justice Department Gopher	gopher://justice2.usdoj.gov:70/1
Justice Information Technology Network	http://www.nlectc.org/
The Department of the Treasury Services	http://www.ustreas.gov:80/treasury/services/services.html
U.S. Government and Law	
Criminal Justice–Country Reports	gopher://UACSC2.ALBANY.EDU:70/11/newman//crjdoc
U.S. Federal Register	http://www.best.gdb.org/repos/fr/fr-intro.html
Criminal Justice on StateSearch	http://www.state.ky.us/agencies/nasire/STtemp.html
THOMAS: U.S. Legislative Information	http://www.thomas.loc.gov/
P-LAW Legal Resource Locator	http://www.dorsai.org/p-law
CRIMINAL INTELLIGENCE SITES	
Project on Intelligence Reform	http://www.fas.org/irp/
Criminal Intelligence Service Canada/Service Canadien de renseignements criminels	http://www.cisc.gc.ca/explorer.html
Loyola Homepage on Strategic Intelligence	http://www.loyola.edu/dept/politics/intel.html
Criminal Activities	
Major Areas of RAND Research	http://www.rand.org/areas/biblio.html
Inspection Service Main Menu–Fraud	http://www.usps.gov/websites/depart/inspect/
Proceeds of Crime & Money Laundering	http://www.cisc.gc.ca/proceed.html
How Not to be a Money Launderer	http://www.ourworld.compuserve.com/homepages/how_not_to_be_a_money_launderer

SITE	URL
Financial Crimes Enforcement Network (FinCEN)	http://www.ustreas.gov/treasury/bureas/fincen/
Network Payment Mechanisms and Digital Cash	http://www.ganges.cs.tcd.ie/mepeirce/project.html
KPMG Canada: Investigation and Security	http://www.kpmg.ca/isi/
1996 Fraud Survey (KPMG Canada)	http://www.kpmg.ca/isi/vl/frsur96e.htm
Smut 'n Stuff	http://www.sunsite.unc.edu/smut.html
National Graffiti Information Network	http://www.WWW.InfoWest.COM:80/NGIN/
Hamilton Police Department Narcotics: Vice Unit	http://www.emporium.turnpike.net/~web265/nvu.htm

ARSON SITES

The Fire Science Centre at the University of New Brunswick	http://www.fsc.unb.ca/
Networked Resources for Fire Protection	http://www.nafed.org/

ORGANIZED CRIME

WLR Cassidy & Associates	http://users.deltanet.com/~wcassidy/wirc/wlcindex.html
MotherJones MJ95:The New Mafia Order	http://www.mojones.com/mother-jones/MJ95/viviano.html

Gambling

Wiretap Articles on Gaming	gopher://wiretap.spies.com/11/Library/Article/Gaming
Crackdown On Illegal Gambling	http://www.rogers.com/miss/mag/cm994-s.htm
ConJelCo Home Page–Gambling	http://www.conjelco.com/index.html
Jim Feist's Sports & Gaming Update	http://www.jimfeist.com/

Drugs

WWW Drug Information Server (at Paranoia)	http://www.paranoia.com/drugs/
Hyperreal (Drugs)	http://www.hyperreal.com/drugs/
HempBC's Online Catalog	http://www.hempbc.com/virtual_store/storemain.html
Drug Text USA	http://www.drugtext.org/drugtext.html
Cannabis Canada–The Magazine of...	http://www.hempbc.com/magazine/magmain.html
Marijuana Growers	http://www.hyperreal.com/drugs/marijuana/growers/index.html
Information on Cannabis	http://www.magic.mb.ca/~lampi/drugs/cannabis.html
Marijuana Policy Project	http://www.mpp.org/
International Narcotics Control Board	http://www.undcp.or.at/incb_hp.html
UNDCP Home Page	http://www.undcp.org/index.html
Annual Report–Cooperation for Development: Other Entities	http://www.oas.org/EN/PINFO/arotrae.htm#sub
Hemp Initiatives Projects of Washington State (HIP-WS)	http://www.hemp.net/hipws/hipws.html

SITE	URL
MISSING KIDS SITES	
RCMP Missing Children's Registry	http://www.childcybersearch.org/
National Centre for Missing and Exploited Children	http://www.missingkids.org/
SAFE-T-CHILD Online	http://www.yellodyno.safe-t-child.com/
COMMUNITY, YOUTH AND GANGS	
Crime and Law Enforcement (Community)	http://galaxy.einet.net/galaxy/Community/Crime-and-Law-Enforcement.html
Crime Responsibility and Youth (CRY)	http://www2.deepcove.com/cry/
Chicago Crime Commission–Gangs	http://www.acsp.uic.edu/oicj/other/cccgangs.htm
DOMESTIC VIOLENCE	
SafetyNet Domestic Violence Resources	http://www.cybergrrl.com/dv.html
Caveat (Canadians Against Violence)	http://www.caveat.org/
Partnerships Against Violence (PAVNET)	http://www.usdoj.gov/pavnet.html
Assault Prevention Information Network Index	http://galaxy.einet.net/galaxy/Community/Safety/Assault-Prevention/apin/APINindex.html
EMERGENCY SERVICES SITES	
Emergency Services WWW Sites	http://gilligan.uafadm.alaska.edu/WWW-911.htm
Allied Agencies	http://www.oes.ca.gov:8001/html/allies.html
WAR AND PEACE SITES	
War and Peace Resources	http://www.intac.com/PubService/human_rights/LIST/war.html
PeaceNet	gopher://gopher.igc.apc.org/11/peace/
Partnerships for Peace	http://www.nato.int/pfp/pfp.htm
United States Institute of Peace	http://www.usip.org/
Information Resources Centre–DND	http://www.cfcsc.dnd.ca/
MILNET: Terrorist Groups	http://www.milnet.com/milnet/tgrps.htm
Balkans–ex–Yugoslavia	gopher://gopher.igc.apc.org:70/11/peace/yugo
STATISTICS SITES	
UNCJIN–Statistics and Research Sources	http://www.ifs.univie.ac.at/uncjin/mosaic/stats.html
Statistics Canada Subject Information	http://www.statcan.ca/Documents/English/Subjects/sub.htm
Welcome to Statistics Canada	http://www.statcan.ca/start.html
U.S. Bureau of Justice Statistics	http://www.ojp.usdoj.gov/bjs/
Home Office–Research and Statistics	http://www.open.gov.uk:80/home_off/rsdhome.htm
Other Statistical WWW Services	http://www.statcan.ca/Reference/otherservers.html

SITE	URL

DAILY NEWS

Commercial News Services on the World Wide Web	http://www.jou.ufl.edu/commres/webjou.htm
PointCast Canada	http://www.pointcast.ca
World News and Other Media	http://www.cfn.cs.dal.ca/Current/WorldNews.html
The Daily News Worldwide	http://www.hfxnews.com//
Canada NewsWire	http://www.newswire.ca/
GLOBEnet	http://www.globeandmail.ca/
Financial Post	http://www.canoe.ca/FP/home.html
Canadian Corporate News	http://www.cdn-news.com
Canadian News Headlines	http://www.radio.cbc.ca/radio/programs/news/headline-news
Maclean's	http://www.canoe.ca/macleans/home.html
CBC Newsworld Online	http://www.newsworld.cbc.ca
Pointcast Network Canada	http://athena.theglobeandmail.com/pointcast/
Toronto Star	http://www.thestar.com
The Globe and Mail	http://www.globeandmail.ca
Halifax Daily News	http://www.hfxnews.com/
China News Digest	http://www.cnd.org:8000/
Interactive Age Daily	http://techweb.cmp.com/ia/dailies/daily.htm
CBS News: UTTMlink	http://uttm.com/
Public Weather Forecasts	http://www.on.doe.ca/text/text_index.html
The News	http://www.peinet.pe.ca/news.html
The Ottawa Citizen Online Home Page	http://www.ottawacitizen.com/
CNN Interactive	http://www.cnn.com/
Today's Birthday	http://www.eb.com/calendar/calendar.html

E-ZINES

John Labovitz's e-zine list	http://www.meer.net/~johnl/e-zine-list/
Welcome to PC World Online!	http://www.pcworld.com/home/index.phtml

CANADIAN SITES

Canadian-based Information Systems	http://www.cs.cmu.edu/afs/cs.cmu.edu/user/clamen/misc/Canadiana/CA-gophers.html
Canada Net Pages	http://www.cyberion.com/canadanet/
Canadian WWW Central Index/Liste centrale des serveurs WWW canadiens	http://www.csr.ists.ca/w3can/Welcome.html
Canadiana–The Canadian Resource Page	http://www.cs.cmu.edu/Web/Unofficial/Canadiana/README.html
Champlain: Canadian Information Explorer	http://info.ic.gc.ca/champlain/champlain.html

SITE	URL
Government of Canada/Gouvernement du Canada	http://canada.gc.ca/
Open Government–Gouvernement Ouvert	http://info.ic.gc.ca/opengov/
Department of Foreign Affairs and International Trade	http://www.dfait-maeci.gc.ca
List of Canadian Missions Abroad	http://dfait-maeci.gc.ca/english/html/60/60001.htm
Parliamentary Business and Publications	http://www.parl.gc.ca/english.ebus.html
Master Parliamentary Committee Page	http://www.parl.gc.ca/cgi-bin/committees352/english_master.pl
Treasury Board of Canada / Conseil du Trésor du Canada	http://www.tbs-sct.gc.ca/
Transport Canada	http://www.tc.gc.ca/nov1_96/index_e.htm
Government Information Finder Technology (GIFT)	http://www.gc.ca/home.html
Auditor General Report '95	http://www.gc.ca/oag_95/oag95/homepage.html

LIBRARY RELATED SITES

Canadian Government Libraries	gopher://gopher.nlc-bnc.ca:70/11gopher%24root%3A%5Bsites.gov-gouv.federal.lib-bib.eng%5D
Criminal Justice Libraries	gopher://UACSC2.ALBANY.EDU:70/11/newman//wcjln/cjlib
Centre of Criminology Library–U of T	http://library.utoronto.ca/www/libraries_crim/crimhome.htm
Department of the Solicitor General–Library	http://www.sgc.gc.ca/~library/
National Library of Canada	http://www.nlc-bnc.ca/ehome.htm
Bibliothèque nationale du Québec	http://www.biblinat.gouv.qc.ca/
Librarians' Home Page Directory	http://www.he.net/~libdir/index.html
Library of Congress	http://www.loc.gov/
Canadian Library Association	http://www.cla.amlibs.ca/
CASLIS	http://www.ualberta.ca/~thornley/caslis.html
Council of Federal Libraries	http://www.nlc-bnc.ca/cfl-cbgf/

Reference

Welcome to the Electric Library	http://www2.elibrary.com/search.cgi
Gopher Jewels	gopher://cwis.usc.edu:70/11/Other_Gophers_and_Information_Resources/Gopher-Jewels
IPL The Internet Public Library	http://ipl.sils.umich.edu/
The Virtual Reference Desk	http://thorplus.lib.purdue.edu/reference/index.html
NetFirst Home Page	http://www.oclc.org/oclc/netfirst.htm

Online Search Services

Dialog Home Page	http://www.dialog.com/
ERIC/ChESS Home Page	http://www.indiana.edu/~ssdc/eric-chess.html

SITE	URL
Infomart DIALOG Home Page	http://www.infomart.ca/
Micromedia Limited–What's New	http://www.mmltd.com/files/whats_new/whats_new.html
QUICKLAW Home Page	http://www.qlsys.ca/
ASISNET (private security database)	http://www.asisonline.org
SilverPlatter World	http://www.silverplatter.com/

Document Delivery

EBSCOdoc Home Page	http://www.ebscodoc.com/
CISTI home page	http://www.cisti.nrc.ca/cisti/
National Library of Canada–Resource Sharing	http://www.nlc-bnc.ca/resource/resha-e.htm

Acquisition and Collection Development

The Weekly Checklist	http://www.ccg-gcc.ca/dsp-psd/Checklist/lists-e.html
EBSCO Information Services Home Page	http://www.ebsco.com/
e-zine-list: Alphabetic Listing	http://www.meer.net/~johnl/e-zine-list/zines/Alpha.html
Consolidated New York–Edison Magazine List	http://www.epa.gov/Region2/library/allmags.htm
Crime Publications Library	http://www.heritage.org/heritage/library/#crime
Addiction Research Foundation Bibliographies	http://www.arf.org/isd/bib/list.html
The Village at Intertain	http://www.intertain.com/
International Thomson Publishing	http://www.thomson.com/
EBSCO Publishing Home Page	http://www.epnet.com/
Information Access Company Homepage (Ziff Davis)	http://www.iacnet.com/
HMSO Home Page	http://www.hmso.gov.uk/

Library and Information Science

Library and Information Science	http://www.phoenix.ca/library/lis/index.html
Newsgroup:bit.listserv.autocat	news:bit.listserv.autocat
International Federation of Library Associations and Institutions (IFLA)	http://www.nlc-bnc.ca/ifla/
Research Libraries Group Home Page	http://www-rlg.stanford.edu/welcome.html

DISTANCE LEARNING SITES

Videoconferencing for Learning	http://www.kn.pacbell.com/wired/vidconf/vidconf.html/

NATIVE AND ABORIGINAL SITES

NativeWeb Home Page	http://web.maxwell.syr.edu/nativeweb/
Native American Home Pages	http://info.pitt.edu/~lmitten/indians.html
Aboriginal Super Information Hwy	http://Alpha.Remcan.Ca/abinfohwy/
Indian and Northern Affairs Canada/ Affaires indiennes et du Nord Canada	http://www.inac.gc.ca/

SITE	URL

HUMAN RIGHTS SITES

Human Rights Gopher	gopher://gopher.humanrights.org:5000/
University of Minnesota Human Rights Library	http://www.umn.edu/humanrts/
Human Rights Resources	http://www.intac.com/PubService/human_rights/ LIST/hr_res.html
Human Rights Related Issues	http://www.intac.com/PubService/human_rights/ LIST/rel.html
Church of Euthanasia Home Page	http://www.paranoia.com/coe/
American Civil Liberties Union	http://www.aclu.org/

HEALTH AND SAFETY SITES

OSHWEB–Index of Occupational Safety and Health Resources	http://turva.me.tut.fi/~oshweb/
ILO-CIS–International Occupational Safety and Health Information Centre	http://turva.me.tut.fi/cis/home.html
CCOHS Home Page	http://www.ccohs.ca/
NIH Home Page (National Institutes of Health)	http://www.nih.gov/

BUSINESS AND INDUSTRY

Business Resources on the Internet	http://www2.inforamp.net/iramp/inforamp/business/
Spirit: Canadian Electronic Content	http://www.bccc.com/Spirit/Spirithome.html
Ottawa Citizen Online–Classified Advertising	http://www.ottawacitizen.com/advertising/classified.html
KPMG Canada: Insurance Practice	http://www.kpmg.ca/insure/
Insurance Canada Directory	http://www.insurance-canada.ca/insurcan/assoc.htm
Insurance Bureau of Canada	http://www.ibc.ca
RISKWeb–The RISKNet World Wide Web Server	http://www.riskweb.com/riskweb.html
IBM SecureWay	http://www.ibm.com/security/
The World Bank Home Page	http://www.worldbank.org/
Royal Bank of Canada / Banque Royale du Canada	http://www.royalbank.com/
Banking in the Russian Federation	http://www.garant.ru/info/english/rbanks.html
United States Postal Service Public WWW Server	http://www.usps.gov/
Downtown Anywhere–Front Street	http://www.awa.com/index.html
Canada Stockwatch frames	http://www.canada-stockwatch.com/
NETworth Quote Server	http://quotes.galt.com/
Montreal Exchange	http://www.telenium.ca/MSE/e.html
TSE Quotes	http://www.telenium.ca/TSE/index.html
Vancouver Stock Exchange	http://www.vse.com/

SITE	URL
Canadian Company Law Digest	http://www.res.com/`talou/preface.htm
Canadian Directory of Professionals	http://www.cadvision.com/Home_Pages/accounts/ nodrickb/directory.html
Canadian Internet Business Directory	http://www.cibd.com
Canadian Financial Network	http://www.canadianfinance.com
Annual Report Source	http://www.annualreport.com/CyberPlex/ARS/ AnnualReportSource.html

OTHER SITES

National Capital Freenet/Libertel de la Capitale nationale	http://www.ncf.carleton.ca/
Canada411 Phone Directory	http://canada411.sympatico.ca/
Fast Area Code Look-Up	http://www.555-1212.com/aclookup.html
Directory of Canadian Embassies, Consulates, and Trade Offices	http://www.dfait-maeci.gc.ca/english/trade/menu.htm
United States Information Service: Ottawa	http://www.usis-canada.usia.gov/usis.htm
Canada Post Corporation Home Page	http://www.mailposte.ca
Federal Express Official Home Page	http://www.fedex.com
Purolator Courier Official Home Page	http://www.purolator.com
United Parcel Service Official Home Page	http://www.ups.com
Windows95 Annoyances	http://www.creativelement.com/win95ann/

Travel and Tourism

Public Weather Forecasts	http://www.on.doe.ca/text/text_index.html
Canadian Airlines International Ltd.	http://www.CdnAir.ca/
Air Canada	http://www.aircanada.ca/profile.html
FH: Canada Travel Home Page	http://www.fleethouse.com/fhcanada/fhc_expl.htm
Digital Tour of Ottawa	http://www.digimark.net:80/iatech/tour/
WebLouvre: Bienvenue!	http://www.sunsite.unc.edu/louvre/

Entertainment

The Discovery Channel Canada	http://www.discovery.ca/
The CBC Homepage	http://www.cbc.ca/
Ultimate TV List	http://www.tvnet.com/UTVL/utvl.html
Disney–Disney.com Home Page	http://www.disney.com/

Cities and Countries Worldwide

United Nations and other international organizations	http://www.undcp.org/unlinks.html
United Nations Gopher	gopher://nyworkl.undp.org/
Country Studies/Area Handbooks	http://www.leweb2.loc.gov/frd/cs/cshome.html
City.Net	http://www.city.net/
Ottawa Area Sources on the Web	http://www.synapse.net/~radio/ottawa.htm

SITE	URL
ANU–Useful Asian Studies Resources	http://coombs.anu.edu.au/WWWVLPages/AsianPages/WWWVL-AsianUseful.html
Burkina Faso Page	http://www.sas.upenn.edu/African_Studies/Country_Specific/Burkina.html
Rwanda Page	http://www.sas.upenn.edu/African_Studies/Country_Specific/Rwanda.html
IRAN related WWW/Gopher/FTP Sites	http://tehran.stanford.edu/other.html
News from the Czech Republic	http://www.columbia.edu/~js322/czech.html
Foreign Language Resources	http://www.itp.berkeley.edu/~thorne/HumanResources.html

Transportation

Air Canada Home Page	http://www.aircanada.ca
Airlines on the WWW	http://haas.berkeley.edu/~seidel/airline.html
Canadian Passenger Rail Home Page	http://www.mcs.net/~dsdawdy/Canpass/canpass.html
Greyhound Canada	http://www.greyhound.ca/
Voyageur Colonial Bus Lines	http://voyageur.com/infoe.htm

FINDING IT ON THE INTERNET

MetaCrawler Searching (multiple engines)	http://www.metacrawler.com/
Deja News–The Source for Internet Newsgroups	http://www.dejanews.com/
Netscape Home Page	http://home.netscape.com/
Yahoo Search	http://www.yahoo.com/search.html
WebCrawler Searching	http://www.webcrawler.com/
Open Text Corporation	http://www.opentext.com/
AltaVista: Main Page	http://www.altavista.digital.com/
Your Excite Live!	http://www.home.excite.com/
Point Communications Corporation	http://www.pointcom.com/
Search the Magellan	http://www.mckinley.com/
InfoSeek Home Page	http://www2.infoseek.com/
Lycos	http://a2z.lycos.com/
WWWW–the World Wide Web Worm	http://wwww.cs.colorado.edu/home/mcbryan/WWWW.html
Welcome to ALIWEB	http://web.nexor.co.uk/public/aliweb/aliweb.html
Hytelnet	gopher://liberty.uc.wlu.edu:70/11/internet/hytelnet
Amazing Internet Guide (access various search engines)	http://www.sunstorm.com/amazing/
Frame Search (use multiple search engines simultaneously)	http://www.w3com.com/fsearch/
Government Information Finder Technology (GIFT)	http://www.gc.ca

SITE	URL
Internet Explorer	http://www.eecg.toronto.edu/~bryn/HTML/Explorer.html
SavvySearch	http://www.cs.colostate.edu/~dreiling/smartform.html
Submit It! (register your home page with search catalogs)	http://www.submit-it.com/
Four11 E-Mail Directory Services	http://www.Four11.com/
Whois Gateway	gopher://sipb.mit.edu:70/1B%3AInternet%20whois%20servers
About the Internet	
World-Wide Web Servers: Summary	http://www.W3.org/
Internet Domain Survey	http://www.nw.com/zone/WWW/top.html
Internet Canada News	http://www.bowdens.com/icnews.htm
WORLD: Internet News and Resources	http://www.iworld.com/

SUMMARY

Recent academic literature regarding private security in Canada is lacking. However, despite this limited academic research, the Internet provides a wealth of information that is beneficial to the security industry. There is no doubt that on-line information databases will play an increasingly important role in the security function of the future as we move forward in the information age.

REVIEW QUESTIONS

1. Where was the bulk of the Canadian academic research into private security conducted in the 1970s and early 1980s?
2. How does the Internet help private security practitioners?
3. Will the Internet continue to be a powerful tool for private security practitioners in the future? Explain.

Conclusion

Over the last thirty years the private security industry worldwide has grown dramatically. Canada's security industry is no exception to this trend: Canadian estimates are that the ratio of private security personnel to police (federal, provincial, municipal) is almost 4:1, or 200 000 compared to just under 56 000. There are many reasons to believe that the private security sector will continue to grow. Chief among these are the following:

- Public budgets are being cut, so that police services may not investigate (for example) a corporate fraud below $100 000, because of a lack of resources.
- The public perceives that crime is increasing.
- A large number of people are entering their 50s, who typically are more affluent and better able to afford private security (including alarm systems and gated housing).
- Demographics also suggest that white-collar crimes such as fraud are going to increase, and that this will pose a greater burden for police (see above police cutbacks).

I hope the reader has begun to get a sense of the complexity and diversity of the private security industry. The stereotyped image of a private security professional—a retired male, with little formal education, who does little more than watch entrances and exits—is sometimes still accurate but is definitely no longer considered the norm. Private security today is only limited by one's definition of the term. Security nowadays can mean forensic accountants who specialize in detecting fraud or risk, and managers who try to limit losses of any kind (such as lawsuits and criminal activities). Computer specialists who develop information protection systems, such as encryption/decryption processes and anti-virus programs, can also be considered private security personnel.

With this growth there have arisen many issues and challenges that need to be addressed (see Chapter 2). One of the most important issues facing the private security industry is regulation. Since private security is regulated by the provinces, there are many inconsistencies across Canada in terms of standards (which relate to licensing, training, definitions, and so on). Other issues discussed in this book included the following: access to security, information protection, wages, police/security overlap, and private justice.

Security professionals must have sufficient knowledge of the law (see Chapter 3) to understand their limits and minimize their own liability. In broad terms, they should have at least a general understanding of the following: criminal offences, arrest, detention, Charter applicability, right to counsel, statement collection rules, search, trespass to property, and tort and contract law. Many of these topics are relevant if a security officer is conducting an internal investigation concerning a theft where several employees are being interviewed. Knowledge of these subjects should be mandatory for anyone involved in conducting arrests and/or searches.

Career opportunities (see Chapter 5) will increase in the private security sector. However, the skill level required for security professionals will also increase. There will be less need for the stereotypical guard at his post. Today's security professionals will need to understand what Peter Drucker referred to as the "information-based organization." We live in a technological world in which access to information is no longer distributed only to those at the top of an organization. The information is likely accessible to all. The trend toward decentralization—for example, toward reducing middle management and flattening the organization—is also being seen in private security departments, both contract or in-house. Computers will continue to play an increasingly important role for security professionals in both operational and administrative capacities (that is, in databanks, communications, filing systems, and so on). The availability of security hardware is already reducing the need for "human" guards. For example, one multinational firm monitors its site in Saudi Arabia from Ontario and then notifies Saudi authorities as required.

Continuing education will be an important asset for security professionals, whether it be in traditional law and security/criminology programs, or computer science, or business administration. To remain competitive, security professionals will have to continually upgrade their skills, whether it be through formal academics (that is, at colleges and universities), or through certification from a variety of security associations that exist, or through on-the-job training and experience.

Before you approach a particular company for a position, endeavour to understand exactly where the company fits in the overall industry, and hence its particular needs. If you are beginning a career search in security, do as much background research as possible on prospective organizations and industries. Chapter 5 pointed you toward some tools that will aid you in this preparation; many of them are available in your local library. It is important to keep abreast of current events—especially business news—whether you are looking for opportunities or not. Keeping aware of current events helps you target organizations that may require security services, since most security positions are not advertised. Also remember that regardless of your approach, in every telephone call, letter, and meeting you are always being evaluated. You must treat these processes accordingly.

Chapter 6 provided a snapshot of academic, industrial, and government research into private security in Canada. Most of these reports can be found in libraries, government departments, and security associations. Do not forget the various trade magazines that exist, such as *Canadian Security* and *Security Management*, which will contain much current information. Also provided in this chapter were a host of Internet sites of interest to security professionals.

Table of Cases

Hicks v. Faulkner (1882) Q.B.D. 167 D.C.

Langlois and Bedard v. Cloutier (1990) 74 C.R. (3d) 316 (S.C.C.)

Boudreau v. The King (1949) 94 C.C.C. 1 (S.C.C.)

Yarmine v. Gustafson (1989) 15 A.C.W.S. (3d) 455 (B.C.C.C.)

Northcott v. Johnson et al. (1982) 18 A.C.W.S. (2d) 238 (Ontario Small Claims Ct.)

Gilchrist v. Raymond Lee Pharmacy Ltd. (1988) 11 A.C.W.S. (3d) 192 (Ont. High Ct. of Justice)

Freeman v. West Vancouver (District) (1991) 24 A.C.W.S. (3d) 936 (B.C.S.C.)

R. v. Therens (1985) 18 C.C.C. (3d) 481 (S.C.C.)

R. v. Collins (1987) 33 C.C.C. (3d) 1 (S.C.C.)

R. v. J.A. (1992) 'unpublished' Ontario Unified Family Court

R. v. Shafie (1989) 47 C.C.C. (3d) 27 (Ont. C.A.)

R. v. MacDonald (1974) 22 C.C.C. (2d) 350 (N.S.C.A)

R. v. Lerke (1986) 24 C.C.C. (3d) 129 (Alb. C.A.)

R. v. Dean (1991) 5 C.R. (4d) 176 (Ont. Ct. of Justice)

R. Wills (1992) 70 C.C.C. (3d) 529 (Ont. C.A.)

R. v. Brydges (1990) 53 C.C.C. (3d) 380 (S.C.C.)

R. v. Clarkson (1986) 25 C.C.C. (3d) 207 (S.C.C.)

R. v. Letendre (1979) 46 C.C.C. (2d) 398 (B.C.C.A.)

R. v. Wills (1992) 70 C.C.C. (3d) 529 (Ont. C.A.)

Bibliography

Albanese, J. (1986). "The Future of Policing: A Private Concern." *Police Studies.* Vol. 9(2): 86–91.

Amirault, E., and M. Archer (1988). *Canadian Business Law* (3d). Scarborough, Ont.: ITP Nelson.

Angus Reid Group (1992). *Law Enforcement and Private Security: A Public Perspective* (The Chapman Report). Canadian Society For Industrial Security.

Asbury, K. (1988). *Emerging Trends in the Private Security Industry.* Toronto: Sheridan College Press.

——— (1990). "Private Security, Public Police and Mass Residential Space: A Case Study." *Canadian Police College Journal.* 14(1): 1–27.

Bilek, A., J. Kotter, and R. Federal (1983). "Relationships Between Private and Security and Public Force." *Police Work.* 1983: 47–61.

Bocklet, R. (1990). "Police—Private Security Cooperation." *Law and Order.* Dec.: 54–59.

Broder, J.F. (1984). *Risk Analysis and the Security Survey.* Newton, Mass.: Butterworth-Heinemann.

Burstein, Harvey (1996). *Security: A Management Perspective.* Englewood Cliffs, N.J.: Prentice Hall.

——— (1994). *Introduction to Security.* Englewood Cliffs, N.J.: Prentice Hall.

CACP (1994). *Prevention of Crime in Industry Committee Report— Public/Private Policing Partnerships: A Model for Implementation.*

Campbell, G., and B. Reingold (1994). "Private Security and Public Policing in Canada." Juristat: Service Bulletin. Vol. 14(1).

Committee on Education and Labor House of Representatives. (1993). Hearings Regarding Private Security Guards. Washington, D.C.: U.S. Government Printing Office.

Cunningham, W., and T. Taylor (1985). *Private Security and Police in America* (The Hallcrest Report). Portland Oregon: Chancellor Press.

Cunningham, W., J. Strauchs, and C. VanMeter (1990). *Private Security Trends 1970–2000* (The Hallcrest Report II). McLean, Va.: Butterworth-Heinemann.

Cunningham, W., and J. Strauchs (1992). "Security Industry Trends: 1993 and Beyond." *Security Management.* December 1992.

Dance, O. (1990). "To What Extent Could or Should Policing Be Privatized?" *Police Journal.* Vol. 63(4): 288–297.

Dempsey, J. (1996). *An Introduction to Public & Private Investigations.* Suffolk Community College: West Publishing.

Department of Justice, Policing Services (1996). *An Act To Provide For Protective Security Services* (draft). Halifax, N.S.: Nova Scotia Government.

De Waard, J. (1994). *Private Security: Size of Sector, Legislation and Policies in the Netherlands and Europe.* The Netherlands: Ministry of Justice.

Draper, H. (1978). *Private Police.* New Jersey: Humanities Press.

Edwards, G. (1994). "Has the Time Come to Privatize the Police?" *Intersec.* Vol.4(5): 164–166.

Erickson, B. (1993). *Companies In The Toronto Private Contract Security Industry.* Ottawa: Police Policy and Research Division, Solicitor General of Canada.

——— (1993). *People in the Toronto Private Contract Security Industry.* Ottawa: Police Policy and Research Division, Solicitor General of Canada.

Eustace, D. (1994) "Rethinking Contract Security—New Factors Alter the Equation." *Canadian Security.* Vol. 16(7): 24–25.

Feuerverger, A., and C. Shearing (1982). "An Analysis of Prosecution of Shoplifters." *Canadian Journal of Criminology.* 20(2): 273–289.

Freedman, D., and P. Stenning (1977). *Private Security, Police and the Law In Canada.* Toronto: Centre of Criminology, University of Toronto.

Gandy, J. (1978). "Book Reviews." *Canadian Journal of Criminology.* 20(2): 209–210.

Gazette (Montreal) (1993). "Change laws to give (security) guards more protection coroner urges." November 25: A4.

George, B., and M. Button (1994). *The Need For Regulation of the Private Security Industry* (unpublished).

Geva, R. (1989). "Cooperation Between the Police and the Private Security and Investigative Industries: The Israeli Survey." *Police Chief.* June 1989: 12,17.

Globe and Mail (1989). "Private eyes not tied by Charter, court rules." February 2: A17.

Hannah, J., O. Ebrahim, and D. Myled (1995). *Case Law For Security Management Selected Offences (1&2).* Ottawa, Ont.: Algonquin College.

Hawkins, D., and E. Konstan (1996). *Canadian Private Investigator's Manual.* Toronto: Emond Montgomery Publications.

Hertig, C. (1986). "Developing Productive Relationships with Private Security." *F.B.I. Law Enforcement Bulletin.* January 1986: 19–22.

Hess, K. and H. Wrobleski (1992). *Introduction to Private Security* (3d.). St. Paul, Minn.: West Publishing.

Hoddinott, J. (1994). "Public Safety and Private Security." *Policing*. Autumn: 158–165.

Home Office (1979). *The Private Security Industry: A Discussion Paper*. London: Her Majesty's Stationery Office.

———(1994). *Review of Police Core and Ancillary Tasks* (interim report). London.

Hsieh, W. (1990). *Law Enforcement and Private Security Executives' Perception of Relationships Between Their Agencies* (thesis). Michigan: Michigan State University.

Independent Committee of Inquiry (1994). *The Role and Responsibilities of the Police* (discussion document). London.

Jayewardene, C., T. Juliani, and C. Talbot (1983). "Private and Special Police." In *The Thin Blue Line—A Historical Perspective of Policing in Canada*. Ottawa: Crimecare: 75–81.

Jefferies, F. (1977). *Private Policing: An Examination of In-house Security Operations*. Toronto: Centre of Criminology, University of Toronto.

——— (1973). *Private Policing: A Bibliography*. Toronto: Centre of Criminology, University of Toronto.

———(ed.) (1973). *Private Policing and Security in Canada: A Workshop*. Toronto: Centre of Criminology, University of Toronto.

John O'Grady Consulting and Radford Game and Associates (1984). *Occupational Standards and Training Needs Analysis*. Toronto, Ont.: Industrial Training Advisory Industrial Adjustment Service Committee.

Johnston, L. (1992). *The Rebirth of Private Policing*. London: Routledge.

Juristat (1996). *Police Personnel and Expenditures in Canada—1994*. Vol. 16, No. 1. Ottawa, Ont.: Statistics Canada.

——— (1995). *Fear and Peronal Safety*. Vol. 15, No. 9. Ottawa: Statistics Canada.

Kaat, B. (1993). "Private Policing: Developments and Consequences for Public Police Forces." *Interpol*. Vol. 443: 24–32.

Kakalik, J., and S. Wildhorn (1977). *The Private Police: Security and Danger*. New York: Crane Russak.

Leclair, C., and S. Long (1996). *The Canadian Security Sector: An Overview*. Ottawa: Industrial Adjustment Committee on the Security Sector.

——— (1996). *The Canadian Security Sector: Standards*. Ottawa: Industrial Adjustment Committee on the Security Sector.

Lipson, M. (1975). *On Guard: The Business of Private Security*. New York: The New York Times Book Co.

Lum, M. (1995). *Market Segment Analysis: Security Products*. Industry Canada.

Maki, D. (1988). *The Market for Employment, Personnel and Security*. Vancouver: The Fraser Institute.

Mangan, T., and M. Shanahan (1990). "Public Law Enforcement/Private Security: A New Partnership?" *FBI Law Enforcement Bulletin*. Jan.: 18–22.

Mathews, R. (1989). *Privatizing Criminal Justice*. Los Angeles: Sage.

McIntyre, J. (1991). *Special Provincial Constables: A Plan for Accountability*. British Columbia: B.C. Police Commission.

Mitchell, M., and W. McGrath (eds.) (1981). *Police Function in Canada*. Toronto: Methuen.

Mollard, M., R. MacKay, and A. Taylor (1993). *Report on the Regulation of the Private Security Industry in British Columbia*. B.C.: Commission of Inquiry—Policing in British Columbia.

Morn, F. (1982). *The Eye That Never Sleeps: A History of the Pinkerton National Detective Agency*. Bloomington: Indiana University Press.

Moylan, J., and R. Pitre (1996). *The Canadian Security Sector: Training & Education*. Ottawa: Industrial Adjustment Committee on the Security Sector.

Moulton, R. (1987). "Should Private Security Have Access to Criminal Conviction Files?" *Police Chief*. June 1987: 35.

Nalla, M., and G. Newman (1991). "Public Versus Private Control: A Reassessment." *Journal of Criminal Justice*. Vol. 19(6): 537–547.

National Advisory Committee on Criminal Justice Standards and Goals. (1976). *Private Security: Report of the Task Force on Private Security*. Washington. D.C..

Normandeau, A., and B. Leighton (1990). *A Vision of the Future of Policing in Canada: Police Challenge 2000*. Ottawa: Minister of Supply and Services Canada.

Private Investigators and Security Guards Act, R.S.O., 1990.

Private Security Advisory Council (1976). *A Report on the Regulation of Private Security Guard Services*. Washington, D.C.: The American Society for Industrial Security.

Ray, D. (1993). *Canadian Private Security Law*. Calgary: Cross Publishing.

———(1995). *Canadian Private Security: Administration*. Calgary: Cross Publishing.

Report on the Proceedings of the Canadian Conference of the Security Industry (1992). Held in Ottawa.

Robbins, D.A. (1989). *Report to the Strategic Planning Committee on the Private Security Industry in Ontario*. Ontario Provincial Police.

Robinson, R. (1993). "Private Investigation Is a Grey Area That Requires Continued Surveillance." *Canadian Security*. April/May: 17.

Sennewald, C. (1985). *Protection Officer Training Manual, What Every Officer Must Know*. Cochrane, Alta: Protection Officer Publications.

———(1996). *Security Consulting* (2d ed.). Newton, Mass.: Butterworth-Heinemann.

Shearing, C., M. Farnell, and P. Stenning (1980). *Contract Security in Ontario*. Toronto: Centre of Criminology, University of Toronto.

Shearing, C., and P. Stenning (1979). *Search and Seizure: Powers of Private Security Personnel* (A study prepared for the Law Reform Commission of Canada). Ottawa: Ministry of Supply and Services.

———— (1981) "Modern Private Security: Its Growth and Implications." In M. Tonry and N. Morris (eds.), *Crime and Justice—An Annual Review of Research*, Vol. 3. Chicago: University of Chicago Press. 193–245.

———— (1982). *Private Security and Private Justice: The Challenge of the 80's (A Review of Policy Issues)*. Brookfield Vt.: Brookfield Publishing.

———— (1982). "Snowflakes or Good Pinches—Private Security's Contribution to Modern Policing." In R. Donelan (ed.), *The Maintenance of Order in Society*. Ottawa: Canadian Police College. 96–105.

———— (1983). "Private Security: Implications for Social Control." *Social Problems*. 30(5): 493–506.

———— (1984). "From the Panopticon to Disney World: The Development of Discipline." In A. Doob and E. Greenspan (eds.), *Perspectives in Canadian Law*. Aurora: Canadian Law Books Co. 335–349.

———— (eds.). (1987) *Private Policing*. Newbury Park, Ca: Sage.

Shearing, C., P. Stenning, and S. Addario (1985). "Public Perception of Private Security." *Canadian Police College Journal*. Vol. 9(3): 225–253.

Stenning, P., and C. Shearing (1980). "The Quiet Revolution: The Nature, Development and General Legal Implications of Private Security in Canada." *Criminal Law Quarterly*. Vol. 22(2): 220–248.

Smith, K., and R. Prouse (1987). *Canadian Private Security Manual*. Toronto: Carswell.

Solicitor General Canada (1986). "Cooperative Policing: The Way of the Future?" *Liaison*. Vol. 12(1): 9–12.

———— (1986) "Crime Prevention: A Sound Business Investment." *Liaison*. Vol. 12(8): 18–24.

South, N. (1988). *Policing for Profit*. London: Sage.

Spitzer, S., and S. Scull (1977). "Privatization and Capitalist Development: The Case of the Private Police." *Social Problems*. Vol. 25(1): 18–29.

Stansfield, R. (1996). *Issues in Policing: A Canadian Perspective*. Toronto: Thompson Educational Publishing.

Stenning, P., and M. Cornish (1975). *The Legal Regulation and Control of Private Security In Canada* (working paper). Toronto: Centre of Criminology, University of Toronto.

Stenning, P. (1989). "Private Police and Public: Toward a Redefinition of the Police Role." In D. Loree (ed.), *Future Issues in Policing*. Symposium Proceedings. Ottawa: Canadian Police College. 169–192.

The Steering Committee National IAS for the Security Sector (1996). *Report of the Second Conference of the Canadian Security Sector*. Industrial Adjustment Committee on the Security Sector.

Trofymowych, D. (1993). *Private Policing in Canada, A Review* (unpublished report). Ottawa: Police Policy and Research Division, Solicitor General of Canada.

Trojanowicz, R., and B. Bucqueroux (1990). "The Privatization of Public Justice: What Will It Mean to Police?" *Police Chief*. October: 131–135.

Tyska, L., and L. Fennelly (1987). *Security in the Year 2000*. California: ETC Publications.

University of Toronto (1973). *Private Policing and Security in Canada: Selected Readings for a Workshop.* Toronto: Centre of Criminology.

Wanat, J., E. Guy, and J. Merrigan (1981). Supervisory Techniques for the Security Professional. Boston: Butterworth Publishers.

West, M. (1992). "Privatizing Nonessential Police Services: Future Impact On Law Enforcement." *Journal of California Law Enforcement*. Vol. 26(4).

Winnipeg Free Press (1994). "Crime spurs residents to hire private security." July 4: B1.

Index